Church Computing: A Strat

Church Computing:
A Strategy

Gareth Morgan
MA[Comp Sci], BA[Theol], MBCS

Jay books

Jay books
Woodside, Hadlow Park, Hadlow, Tonbridge, Kent TN11 0HZ, England

First published 1987
© Gareth G Morgan 1987

British Library Cataloguing in Publication Data

Morgan, Gareth G.
   Church computing : a strategy.
   1. Church management—Data processing
   I. Title
   262'.0028'5   DV652.77

   ISBN 1-87040-402-5

Cover design by Jenny Clouter
Photoset by MC Typeset Ltd, Chatham, Kent
Printed by Whitstable Litho Printers Ltd, Whitstable, Kent

Contents

Foreword ――――――――――――――――

by Monica Hill, executive secretary of the British Church Growth Association

Computers are tools which the modern world has learned to use effectively in many different ways but which the church has neglected and felt to be alien in the mission of Christ.

Gareth Morgan has made a significant contribution to bringing the management of British churches into the twentieth century, not only with his pioneering work in producing relevant software, but also first with his practical help and advice to churches through Kubernesis, and now through this book.

For too long the church has retained nineteenth century methods in many areas of its mission and administration. Christian leaders have been afraid to use modern technology which in secular and commercial fields is considered essential. Thus the church is denied the aids that could increase the efficiency of its pastoral care and evangelism as well as its basic sharing of church information. We are often so concerned to prevent the world from entering the church that we create barriers that prevent the church entering the world.

I too have been at fault here. Although I have always been interested in the elementary mathematical logistics behind computers, I have tended to see them as being mainly for young people who have grown up with then. There are many Christian leaders who feel they can manage reasonably well with the methods and resources that have been used for generations. But if we ignore the technology of our age we may be blocking what God has provided to release ministries and give increase to the outreach of the Gospel today.

The invitation to write this Foreword came at the same time as a decision taken by the Council of the British Church Growth Association to computerise its administration and the recognition on my part that theory would need to turn into practice! The Lord moves in mysterious ways to achieve his purposes and I have greatly benefited by studying this book which so able sets the background steps to be taken to using a computer in the work of the church.

This is not a technical book; its emphasis is practical. It sets out the steps that can be taken by any local church whose leaders are tired of putting up with outdated impractical administration. Computers can make the difference between simple organised efficiency and simple disorganised chaos.

A good computer system can save the church untold hours of time and money. But we are reminded that computers are only as good as the commitment to make them work and the material put into them. 'GIGO' is an appropriate computer term – 'Garbage In, Garbage Out'. A little time spent in careful planning can make the system work *for* you rather than your being a slave to it.

Gareth Morgan's experience of thirteen years in the computer field, five of which have been specialising in church computer work, has been put to good use in this book. His experience of church consultancies through Kubernesis and his Senior Lecturership in Computer Studies at Bristol Polytechnic make him one of the foremost experts in this field in Britain.

This book is a 'must' for the local church. In it Gareth Morgan has shown how modern scientific technology can serve the mission of Christ.

Note on terminology

Throughout this book, the terms *ministers* and *clergy* are used inter-changeably to refer to priests, pastors, or senior church leaders in any Christian denomination. Similarly the terms *local church* and *parish* are used to describe a church community and those it serves, regardless of denomination. The term *members* refers to all those who are involved in the local church on a committed basis. The term *church council* is used to indicate the main decision making body of the local church.

Computer jargon has been avoided as far as possible, but occasionally technical terms are needed simply to describe computer systems in use. A glossary will be found at the end, which may be of assistance to readers new to the field.

Mention of specific products, with all the acronyms and model numbers these involve, has been kept to a minimum and, where essential, confined to footnotes for the benefit of those interested in this information.

Preface

This book derives from two basic convictions. The first is that Christianity makes no sense without a doctrine of the Church, and that within any doctrine of the Church, the role of the local church is vital. The second is that a properly chosen and properly applied computer system can offer enormous benefits for almost any organisation, and those who ignore its potential are overlooking what is probably the most important tool of the late twentieth century.

In suggesting a *strategy* for church computing, I have attempted to set some guidelines for churches and individual clergy who wish to consider what place a computer may have in church life. Although chapters 2 and 3 are devoted to computer applications and the selection of systems to run them, the majority of the text is about the local church itself, considering *how* and *why* a computer system should play a part, and what practical steps a church should take to ensure a dependable system.

The strategy that is offered is not based on proven research, but more on five years of practical involvement with churches considering computer systems, looking at their needs, seeking to produce software that would be of real service, and attempting to offer help if problems arose. In that time, it has become clear that some churches have gained much more benefit from their computers than others, and my aim in this book is to suggest criteria that will increase the likelihood of a church achieving a really worthwhile system.

The underlying themes are the need to manage information as a vital church resource, and the central importance of communication within church life. In arguing for the significance of these themes I have attempted to indicate the role that a computer system can have in responding to them. For those who accept that church growth, in all its senses, depends at least in part on good information and communication, this book offers some practical ways to proceed.

Acknowledgements

My greatest thanks must go to the numerous church people, lay and ordained, who have allowed me to work with them in the *Kubernesis* project and to develop most of the ideas on which the book is based. It would be impossible to name all concerned, but I would especially thank those who had the courage to be involved in the early days and those who have a particular vision for the possibilities a church computer can bring.

Special tribute must be paid to Sharon Morgan, my wife and partner in Kubernesis. Much of the work from which the book derives is as much hers as mine, and very little would have been achieved without her involvement in church computing and her support for the book. Parts of certain chapters are based on material previously published as *Kubernesis booklets* and I am grateful to Sharon as co-author for supporting their inclusion in the present text.

I would also wish to express thanks to Stephen Collyer, Charmion Mann, George Mitchell, and David Mulvey for ongoing advice and encouragement; to Nigel Hardcastle and Stoker Wilson for their pioneering work in providing a forum for discussion of church computing; to Monica Hill for her support over many years and for contributing the foreword; to John Truscott for much valuable advice; to Ken Jackson for making the book possible; to Stephen Watson who caused me to examine the whole range of information management in a church context; and to colleagues at Bristol Polytechnic for helpful discussions. I am also grateful to IBM for provision of the photograph used in chapter 3.

Gareth Morgan
St Mary Magdalen's day 1987

1
The place of computing in church life

Throughout history the Church has been at the forefront in using new technology, particularly technology that could assist in recording or distributing information. St Paul used the new possibilities of travel and correspondence opened up by the Roman Empire as the basic mechanism of his mission to the Gentiles. In the fourth century, Christians were largely responsible for the development of velum codices as a more permanent way of recording scripture than the papyrus scroll. In the Middle Ages, the production of the bible was the first major use of printing. Even in the present century, the Church has come to make great use of the telephone, the broadcast media, projectors of all kinds, and more recently, the photocopier and the audio or video cassette player.

It thus comes as no surprise to find that computers are finding their way into church life, at a pace which is becoming more rapid each year. There can be few ministers now who do not know of colleagues using computers of some kind, even if their own church has not yet installed any system.

Yet the effective application of computer systems in church life is not always as obvious as it might seem. The right applications must be selected; appropriate products must be chosen; users of the system must be prepared for changed ways of working; and others in church life must understand the new opportunities that the computer can bring in the management of information and the improvement of communication.

We begin by examining the developments that have led to the current extent of computing in the local church.

A brief history

The idea of using computers for church work can be traced back many years. In the 1960s the central offices of the main Christian denominations were beginning to computerise, and even at that time there was anticipation of a day when every local church would have a terminal connected to the central machine, to give instant access to parish records.

The costs of such an arrangement, with all the telecommunication lines required, were and still would be colossal, but fortunately this has not proved necessary. With the emergence of personal computers in the late 1970s and 1980s, it began to be possible to consider a complete computer system at the local church level.

Not only is it much cheaper for each church to have its own computer than to maintain a big central system with thousands of terminals, but a computer system for the local church offers much greater flexibility for service in church life. The church computer is a tool for use in the local situation, with emphasis on pastoral care, effective communication, and efficient administration of church affairs.

Computer enthusiasts who happened to be ministers or church members began to find ways of using microcomputers for church purposes almost as soon as the first machines were on sale. However, these early systems were often based on crudely written amateur programs and complex collections of equipment linked up with numerous wires and cables. Only someone with a sound knowledge of the machine could get the system to work, and even then there is doubt whether the results ever had much benefit in church life – the main benefit was the fun and interest of the hobbyist!

However, this began to change – at least in the United Kingdom – from around 1982. In that year a Church Computer Users Group* was founded, to co-ordinate attempts to apply computing in churches. Also from that date, certain computer consultants and dealers began to take a particular interest in churches as potential users of computers. A small conference organised by the Church Pastoral Aid Society in July 1982 brought together a number of clergy and professionals interested in the effective use of church computing. In the autumn of 1982 one minister conducted a survey across parishes

*The Church Computer Users Group published its first newsletter in April 1982.

in five dioceses to establish congregational attitudes to the possible use of computers. Of the church members surveyed, he found that as many as 63 per cent said they would be unconcerned "if the church kept all its records on computer", so it was clear even then that the idea of computers in church work was a possibility which many found quite acceptable.†

From that point onwards, many churches began thinking seriously about whether computing could offer real advantages in church life, sufficient to justify investment in equipment. For a long while, the majority of church computer users were computer hobbyists, but gradually more and more churches and far sighted ministers began to acquire serious systems specifically for church work. The emphasis began to shift towards reliable systems that could be used by ministers and secretaries without the need for any technical knowledge of computers.

It was clear from early meetings that lack of good quality church software was seen as one of the biggest difficulties. This was eased in 1983 with the launch of the first professionally developed software package specifically for church work,‡ and by 1985 there were at least two firms in the UK supplying church specific software, as well as several dealers offering systems based on general-purpose commercial packages.

The Data Protection Act of 1984 also had a major effect. It forced computer users to take much greater care of their data wherever personal information was involved (see chapter 7). Churches had to rationalise any hobby type systems to ensure they could meet the registration requirements of the Act, and this encouraged a move towards more serious dependable systems.

However, the most significant factor that has led to the widespread use of church computing has been the decreasing costs of computer hardware. In 1983 the minimum cost for a serious system – hardware, software and value added tax – was more than £2000 (even at 1983 prices) and rather more for a large church. Thus many clergy were tempted to try to make do with hobbyist equipment, often based on cassette tapes because disk drives were too expensive, and rarely with any software designed for the job. Many of these were using the BBC microcomputer, or even the home computers developed by Clive Sinclair.

Of those ministers using serious systems at that time, a number said that they felt the computers gave about the same benefit to their

---

†Fernley R. Symons, *Living with computers* report, 1983.
‡Kubernesis Pastoral/Membership System, Version 1, operating on Tandy TRS–80 Model III computers.

ministry as their cars gave. Since the computer cost considerably less than a car, this was considered good value. From 1983 to 1986 increasing numbers of churches or individual ministers took the decision to invest in proper business type computers with appropriate software for their needs. The British made Apricot computers were among the most popular, and the main UK church software firms sold significant numbers of packages for the Apricot range. However, even when the advantages were clearly established, only limited numbers of ministers and churches were able to raise the money required.

The big change came late in 1985 when the consumer electronics giant Amstrad launched a complete disk-based word processing system (with printer and software) for less than £500*, and although this could not run the church specific software packages available, large numbers of clergy purchased this machine to prepare their sermons, correspondence, and newsletters. The time savings they found and the relative ease with which machines could be used convinced even the most dubious that computing had a role in church life.

By late 1986 several manufacturers had brought out low cost computers that could run the same software as the IBM Personal Computer†, which by then had become a standard for serious microcomputer applications. It was now relatively straightforward for the specialist firms offering church software packages to make them available on hardware that was both designed for serious applications and priced moderately.

The increasing numbers of users also led to falling software prices as development costs could be shared amongst greater numbers of purchasers. The overall effect was to bring the cost of a complete church system based on well designed hardware and software below £1000, and hence within the reach of almost any church that could see the benefits to be gained.

Since then, the continuing trend of falling hardware prices (or of more sophisticated products at the same price) coupled with a wider range of applications served by church specific software packages, has opened up even more possibilities for the use of the computers as a vital tool in church life.

The church computer as a tool

There are two extreme views of church computers, and both are

*The Amstrad PCW 8256 was launched in September 1985.
†For example the Amstrad PC 1512, which was launched in September 1986.

equally misleading. One view sees the computer as the panacea for all evils, the technological answer to all prayers, which would run the parish single handedly given the chance. The other sees the computer as a complex piece of equipment, usable only by the initiated, liable to create all kinds of mischief unless carefully contained.

Both these views arise from a misunderstanding of technology. One of the earliest pieces of technology must have been the spade or hoe used to till the soil. We naturally call such an item a tool, as its purpose is to ease the task in hand: it neither takes over the task completely, nor does it present a threat unless deliberately abused as a weapon.

The church computer likewise is a tool: a tool to assist the minister in his or her work, a tool to support the overall functioning of the life of the church. Like all tools it can be used well or badly. As a tool it will not run the church on its own. What it will do is make it possible to carry out much that would have been almost impossible without it, and save time in tasks that were previously very time consuming.

Responsible Christian stewardship demands that the best possible use be made of all resources, not least the time of ministers and leading church members. Few Christians would decline a spade if asked to dig the ground, and similarly, few can genuinely decline the use of a computer system once its role is proven as a tool in church work.

In the remainder of this book we seek to examine the ways in which a computer can be a worthwhile tool in church life, and the steps required to ensure that as a tool it is applied effectively, giving genuine benefits in mission, pastoral work, and administration.

The nature of a church computer system

There are at least three elements to any working computer system: the hardware, the software, and the information processed.

The *hardware* is the actual equipment, the visible part of a system. This consists of a processor, together with various peripheral devices under its control.

The processor is the electronic 'heart' of the system; it has the ability to manipulate information as instructed by a program. Most discussion about the 'microchip' relates principally to the processor, and it was the revolution in microelectronics in the late 1970s that made it possible to construct a microprocessor on a single silicon chip, so that personal computers could be produced at a price level within reach of churches and individuals.

The peripherals usually include devices enabling a human user to put information into the system and get information out: these include a keyboard, a VDU screen, and a printer, as well as devices that can arrange long term information storage, such as disk drives. Most peripherals combine electrical and mechanical operation; for example, a printer responds to electrical signals from the processor, and by mechanical action makes a printed impression on a page.

The *software* consists of the programs which control what the computer actually does. The hardware alone is of no value: it is the software that enables the computer to become a tool for specific tasks. The ability of the processor to carry out very different operations according to the program used makes the computer such a diverse tool, and for some types of computer there are several hundred thousand programs available for various applications. In church work this means that once a computer is acquired, it can be used for several distinct purposes, *provided suitable software is available*. The software will normally be supplied on magnetic diskettes, and accompanied by a manual, but apart from these items it is not really a visible part of the system; its effect is only seen when

A system in use, consisting of computer with two floppy disk drives (see Chapter 3), VDU screen, keyboard and printer.

Church computing

it is running on the computer, accepting information and producing results.

The *information* that the system is to process may be even less visible. It will be stored on magnetic disks, but one is only aware of this when one uses the information to produce a printed listing or to display some details on the screen. The information may consist of church membership records, letters and reports prepared on computer, financial data, and so on. All the information stored will be supplied by the users of the system, using suitable software to accept that information, process it correctly, and generate such outputs as may be required.

At the present time, the hardware of most church computer systems consists of a personal computer (which incorporates the processor, keyboard, screen, and disk drives) connected to a printer which allows the results of processing to be committed to paper. Larger churches may have systems involving several machines. The software will usually involve several distinct application packages to meet different church requirements. These may be used by different people; for example the minister may use a word processing package to prepare sermons and letters, whilst the treasurer may use an accounting package to manage church finances. The information will be unique to each church, and will depend on the choice of software, but virtually all information to be processed by the computer will at some point be stored on magnetic disks.

Information and its management in church life

The increasing use of the term *information technology* to describe computer systems – hardware and software – recognises that the prime function of most systems has little to do with computing in the sense of performing calculations. Rather, the prime function of information technology is to provide a tool for the effective management of information.

The need for effective management of personnel, buildings and other resources in the church is widely accepted, but the need to manage information is more subtle.

However, over the centuries, the management of the central information of the Christian faith, the gospel, has had a very high priority. Only by the most meticulous care were the events of Christ's ministry, death and resurrection collated and transmitted from generation to generation. Until the development of printing, large numbers of monks and scribes devoted their lives to the copying and transmission of biblical manuscripts. Missionaries, evangelists and individual Christians have striven and suffered to offer this information, the message of the good news about Jesus Christ, to all who would hear.

Whilst the gospel is the most important information entrusted to Christians, there is much other information that demands effective management. If the message of the gospel to build up the Church, to visit the sick, to give for those in need, and so on is taken seriously, then as soon as a community reaches any size, the information needed to undertake these tasks is quite considerable. A major pastoral visiting programme cannot be undertaken without systematic records. Money given for church purposes needs careful accounting if it is to be used effectively. If church life is to be deepened, information about activities and decisions must be communicated to all church members.

Computerisation is by no means always the answer, but if the importance of managing church information is accepted, then it follows that the best tools for the job must be considered.

Computer systems are only one item in this. Effective communication of information also depends on appropriate printing and copying facilities, proper use of the telephone for urgent matters, and a willingness to see communication as important in the first place.

Benefits of church computing

The decision to adopt a computer system in church work must not be taken lightly, but the possibilities for church life are enormous. Properly used, the system will make a major difference in many facets of church activity.

Some of the benefits may arise from time saved, particularly in necessary tasks that previously involved laborious paperwork repeated many times. This benefit is important for both ministers and lay people, if it releases them for more effective kinds of service.

However, the greatest advantages are usually in the new things that become possible. The computer system may, for example, make it possible to address individually those items which were previously just left in piles, or it may permit analysis of pastoral needs and membership resources in ways that would previously have been too laborious to be worthwhile. The system may thus serve as a major vehicle towards improving communication in church life.

A more significant benefit may be in terms of outreach. It could be that a computer system with appropriate software might make it possible to produce literature, or distribute newsletters, or organise visiting work, in a way that was never previously possible.

There is also the advantage of greater accuracy of information. Lists and directories which were previously produced yearly, can now be issued much more frequently, simply by using the software to print a listing whenever required. If the computer is seen as the central source of information, and all new and amended details are always recorded on the system, then any listing produced from that information will be the most up to date that is possible.

A suitable system may also be able to produce better management information upon which the church council can take decisions. For example, with a computer accounting system, the treasurer would probably enter the same information as in the former manual books, but having that information on computer may permit financial analysis, comparisons, or projections which would have required disproportionate effort to achieve manually, or which might have been beyond the ability of many treasurers. Similarly, a detailed age and sex breakdown of the church membership might be of great value to a meeting considering church strategy. Such information can be readily obtained from computer records if appropriate software is used, but to compile it manually might be too massive a task.

There will also be many functions which, though they happen without a computer, can be done much better with computer assistance. When any type of document or report is considered, a much better result is usually achieved if word processing is available to allow the document to be edited and revised. Depending on the type of printer attached to the computer, it may also be possible to produce a more attractive result.

In a similar manner, the use of a computer may help to achieve better organisation and more systematic procedures. For example, if arrangements for weddings are handled using a computer, it will usually be necessary to follow certain steps when making plans for each couple, and this can reduce the risk of errors. The same is true of church finance.

Naturally, a computer system cannot turn someone who is by nature disorganised into a paragon of orderliness. If a system requires the regular entry of information and this is not done, the effect of using a computer could serve to increase chaos. But for someone who wishes to be organised, and is willing to follow some sort of procedure, a computer system can help that to be achieved.

In principle, therefore, a properly used computer system offers scope for:

- time saving
- establishment of new ventures
- improvement of communication

- better outreach
- more accurate information
- more extensive information for decision making
- literature of higher quality
- better organisation.

Not all of these benefits would apply in all churches. Whether any of them apply is dependent on the choice of applications and selection of suitable system (see chapters 2 and 3), and on the effective management of the system as a tool in church life (see chapters 8 and 9).

Points of caution

Although significant benefits can result from a computer system in church life, success is by no means guaranteed.

Stories of computer systems that seem to cause more harm than good are frequently quoted, and systems have often failed to meet the initial hopes.

There is no doubt that a badly used or wrongly chosen system can be a major source of aggravation, or worse it can actually lead to a deterioration in church life. Even if there are no specific adverse consequences, it can still be a major waste of money if its fails to produce any benefits.

The study of why systems fail is a complex subject, and sometimes two very similar organisations can select the same hardware and software: in one they prove a major success; in the other they achieve little or nothing.

In a church context it seems that the majority of seriously chosen systems are of benefit, although it can sometimes take longer than anticipated for the benefits to emerge. In those cases where the system has not been successful, it is almost always due to one or more of the following:

- wrong choice of system (hardware and software)

- problems of personnel using the system (e.g. inadequate training or co-ordination, or frequent changes of users)

- lack of commitment to the computer as a major tool (leading to lack of use, or failure to allocate time to use it systematically).

The aim of this book is to help churches to avoid the problems of failed systems, and instead to apply computers as a major item of church strategy, and thereby to achieve significant benefits for their own life, and in the service of Christ and his kingdom.

Points for discussion

1. What do you feel about the concept of *tools* for church work? What other tools does your church use (or need) apart from a computer?

2. What, in your view, has accounted for the rise in use of church computing in the last five years? Do you feel that important new opportunities for church work have arisen?

3. What role could a computer system have in your long term vision for church growth and development?

4. How important is the management of information in the church?

2
Applications _____

To realise the possible benefits of a computer system – through improved communication and better management of information – a church needs to consider very carefully the areas in which a computer will be applied.

This chapter identifies a number of possible computer applications that are relevant in church work. However, these are only examples, and further applications are emerging as churches gain wider experience in using systems.

The possible applications are mainly determined by the availability of suitable software. In most cases, each application for which the computer is to be used will require a separate software package (although in some areas software packages are becoming available which integrate more than one application). The process of choosing software is described in chapter 3, but it must be appreciated that unless software is available, it may not be possible to computerise a particular application. More software is being developed as time proceeds, and the range of possible applications is bound to increase, but a small number of key areas are likely to remain the primary fields of church computing for a good time.

It would be wrong for any one church to attempt to computerise *all* the areas for which software is available – or certainly not all at once. Each church needs to identify perhaps two or three applications where the main benefits will be found, and concentrate on these for at least the first year. If the outcome is satisfactory it may then be worth extending the use of the computer to other church functions.

Word processing

Word processing is simply the use of a computer to prepare documents, edit them, revise them, and print them out in any particular form required.

It is possible to buy machines that are purely word processors, which may be desirable for organisations that do not require other facilities, but for most churches the best solution is to buy a general purpose computer and a word processing software package to run on it. A stand-alone or dedicated word processor is actually constructed as a computer with only one program – a word processing program. By opting for a general purpose computer it is possible to run word processing software and many other applications too.

The word processing program receives text that is typed on the keyboard, together with commands to insert or delete characters, words, or lines. It keeps the document being prepared in electronic form, so insertions and deletions can be handled internally. The user can also move paragraphs or blocks of text around, and control the form in which the document is to be printed (line width, page size, single or double spacing, etc). Word processing packages have a *wraparound* facility, which means that as words are typed the program controls where the lines end and puts words on the next line if there is insufficient room, and when insertions are made all the following words are moved along. Once the user has finished a session of editing or revising a document, it is saved on disk for future use. The word processing program will then print the document onto paper when requested, using the printer attached to the computer. The document can be kept as long as required for further revision, or can be deleted if it will not be needed again.

Word processing can make an enormous difference to churches and to individual clergy, in preparing newsletters, minutes, study material, special orders of service, literature used for outreach, letters, sermons, and many other documents. Often this is the application which occupies the computer for the greatest amount of time.

Sermon preparation can become a new experience, because points can be put down in any order desired and moved around as needed, basic notes can gradually be fleshed out without numerous drafts and redrafts, and finally a full script or set of notes can be printed out in perfect neatness to take into the pulpit. If the same sermon is to be used on another occasion, but with minor variations to allow for a different church or different lectionary readings, these changes can be made quite quickly and a new set of notes printed for the new occasion.

The main advantages of word processing really lie in two areas. It is ideal for producing documents of several pages or more where it is *impossible to get everything right first time*, meaning that a number of drafts are required. In this respect, word processing overcomes the human limitation of typing errors. Once errors are found, they can be corrected and the document reprinted, without the risk of further typing errors being introduced elsewhere. It is also very useful for any document that requires discussion and modification before the text can be finalised.

Word processing is also useful where there are a *number of similar documents to be produced* with large amounts of text in common. This could apply, for example, where several people are to receive broadly the same letter with just a paragraph that differs, or where three sets of sermon notes are required with minor variations in each case.

Some people like to use word processing even for short one-off letters, but in such cases, the benefits over a typewriter are much more modest: it is in the areas mentioned above that the really substantial gains are found.

There are a few areas where the use of word processing can even be a disadvantage. Word processing isolates the user from the detailed control of the position of words on paper, and in most cases it is helpful to be able to leave this to the computer. But for some purposes such as filling in a form, or where half line spaces between paragraphs are used to squeeze a lot of information on to a small piece of paper, the typewriter really has the advantage.

There are many word processing software packages available, and the prices can vary considerably according to the facilities included. On many computers there is a standard word processing package to suit the needs of many users which is available for a fairly modest price or may even be included free with the hardware.

Some of the possible features of word processing packages are considered below. The exact use made by individual churches will vary, and this will determine whether or not to invest in one of the more advanced packages. Consideration must also be given to those who will use the word processing facility. Even the cheapest word processing packages have a wide range of options for producing documents, and in many of the more sophisticated packages the choice of facilities can be daunting for the new user.

Search and replace

Virtually all word processing packages include a search and replace facility which enables the user to change all occurrences of a given word or phrase to another word or phrase. This can occasionally be useful if during revision it is decided to employ a different term to one used previously. For example, in a document one might wish to change all references to *new building* to say *Bishop Henry Building*. Text will be moved along accordingly to accommodate the longer phrase.

The search facility is also useful on its own to locate a particular section for revision in a long document.

Different type styles

All word processing packages allow the user to edit text, but some of the crudest ones provide no facility for controlling features such as underlining, bold print, italics (if available on the chosen printer) and so on. Most users will require at least some facility for this, though the word processing software and the printer must be compatible. See the discussion under *Printers and software* in chapter 3 (page 58).

WYSIWYG

Some word processors claim to offer the advantage of being WYSIWYG (an acronym for *What You See Is What You Get*). The idea is that what appears on the screen is the same as what will appear on the printer, so it is easier for the user to plan layouts. In particular, WYSIWYG word processors usually show the user where pages begin and end while the document is being edited.

It is impossible to divide all word processing packages into those that are WYSIWYG and those that are not; almost all are at least partly WYSIWYG. The problem usually comes with advanced printing features. Few computer screens at ordinary prices can show italics, for example, so this will be highlighted on the screen in some other way, which may require additional characters to be shown. Similarly, the computer screen cannot normally show one-and-a-half line spacing. Moreover, if you line everything up around the page boundaries and then make a major insertion, you will alter where all the page breaks come, so there was little advantage in knowing their position in the first place. The better packages allow one to mark headings in some way so that if they come at the bottom of a page they will be moved on to the next page automatically, which is actually a lot more useful.

WYSIWYG offers some advantages to new users, but once one is familiar with a word processing package it offers little real benefit, and, despite some suppliers' claims, it should not normally be a major factor in choosing word processing software.

Spell checking

A number of word processing packages provide a spelling checker (in some cases as an optional extra). This can be very useful to highlight minor mistakes. The spelling checker contains a substantial dictionary that holds all the most frequent words in the English language. When a document is complete, the spelling checker looks up all the words of the document in its dictionary, and draws the user's attention to all words that are not present.

This will, of course, highlight unusual words and proper nouns, as well as words that are actually spelt or typed wrongly. However, in most cases the user can add extra words to the dictionary, so you can stop it highlighting your own name, the name of your town, and words like *baptism* or *communion* which are common in church work but rare in general.

The size of the dictionary is partly determined by the disk space available. Some of the largest dictionaries can only be used with hard disk computers, and even below that, floppy disk users will have to insert a special dictionary disk to do the spell check, so it is not always best to go for the largest possible dictionary. With anything above 15 000 words, the number of words highlighted is unlikely to be a serious problem. For British use, it is also preferable that the dictionary be based on UK English and not American English.

A spelling checker cannot, of course, spot errors like using *there* when one meant to use *their*, nor can it spot extra or missing words. But it is useful for finding words with the odd letter missed out, and is a valuable addition particularly for people writing reports of any length.

Long documents

Most word processing packages load the document into the computer's internal memory while it is being edited, and this can impose a maximum size on documents that can be handled – a common limit is around 5000 words. Other packages will keep part of the document on disk, and only load the portion required, which means the size of document is limited only by the disk space.

For those involved in writing books or material of similar length, it can be a slight advantage for documents to be as long as desired. No one would write a whole book as one document – a separate document would be used for each chapter – but it can be a little inconvenient if one chapter has to be divided into several documents. On the other hand, the disk based approach does make the system run slower as it takes time to store and retrieve parts of the document on disk.

Columns

Many users are surprised to find that only a few relatively expensive word processing packages will produce text in the form of two or more columns to a page. The reason is that all sorts of technical problems emerge. If text is inserted in one column, what is the effect on the adjacent column? Or how are several columns to be shown on a screen that is only 80 characters wide? It also means that the user has to cope with multiple left and right margins.

In practice, it is much better to include a paste-up stage when multi-column work is involved, particularly for newsletters etc. It is perfectly possible to produce text in a single column as narrow as needed; this can then be cut up and positioned as required on the final page.

This restriction does not prevent one preparing tables that work on rows and columns. That can be done quite simply with tabs, provided the table entries are mostly one line items. Difficulties only arise with producing whole paragraphs in a multi-column format.

Standard text

Many packages allow the user to include standard paragraphs or fixed pieces of text prepared in advance. This is particularly useful for legal work, where standard clauses are frequently required; it is less important in church work, but it could be of value for example to those involved in frequent production of orders of service using standard prayers and hymns. (The latter is, of course, only possible with permission from the relevant copyright holders.*)

Almost all packages provide a means of transferring text from one document to another, but the facilities are sometimes a little cumbersome for frequent use, and a definite facility to include standard text could be helpful to some church users.

Foreign languages

A few word processing packages provide explicit support for use of foreign languages (sometimes at extra cost) with facilities for use of accented letters. This may be valuable to those involved in overseas correspondence, and in the UK to those preparing documents in Welsh (though Welsh users will find difficulty with most systems in adding accents to the letter *w*).

The problem is much more difficult for those who require Greek

*Copyright considerations are discussed succinctly by Eric Thorn in *A Question of Copyright* (Jay books).

for theological work, and even worse if Hebrew is needed. Whilst many matrix printers can be programmed to print special characters created by the software, only with expensive hardware can non-standard characters be displayed on the screen. With Hebrew there is the further problem of moving from right to left. Users who require Hebrew with pointing will meet even more major difficulties.

It is possible to overcome all those problems at a price, and on certain machines with advanced graphics facilities there are special packages available for such purposes. However, if word processing in Greek and Hebrew is the dominant application, it may be necessary to purchase specialist hardware which could not be used for other church applications. Those who really need such facilities should thus seek expert advice before choosing any system. At the time of writing most of the solutions tend to be beyond the means of individual clergy, although they may be viable for theological colleges.

Form letters

A frequently cited use of word processing is for the production of form letters. This facility is also known as *standard letters* or *personalised letters* or as a *mailmerge* option. The idea is that the text of a letter is prepared, with certain information being marked as variable. The variable information usually includes the name and address, the salutation (i.e. the entry after the word *Dear*) and sometimes includes variable text within the body of the letter related to a person's occupation, sex, age, town or other details.

Using a file that contains a list of the relevant names, addresses, and other variable text, the word processing software prints out a fresh copy of the letter for each addressee with appropriate individual details inserted. The letter may then be inserted into a window envelope for dispatch to the person concerned.

The main advantage of this is when one wishes to send a circular letter to a number of people, but achieve more attention than most circulars get. The theory is that if a person receives an individually addressed letter he or she is likely to take more notice than if simply sent a photocopied circular.

Not all word processing packages provide this facility. It is also important that whatever software is used for membership records can link up with word processing to generate form letters: the membership and word processing software must be mutually compatible.

Some word processing packages provide quite advanced facilities to test information and include different paragraphs, for example, according to the person's age or sex, although setting up documents to use these sort of features begins to require skills approaching those needed for computer programming. Even to prepare a form letter in the first place requires quite advanced knowledge of one's word processing package.

There are, however, many snags with the idea of form letters, and whilst they can be useful, their advantages are limited. They can achieve quite an impact when first used, but most people have received so many such letters from firms offering all kinds of special offers, that they cease to have any particular effect.

It is very difficult to word a letter in such a way that recipients each genuinely think it was individually composed to them, and even if this effect is achieved, there is a strong ethical question as to whether churches should attempt such deliberate deceit.

There are also practical problems in that the sort of printers most churches will have connected to their computers can easily take a whole day to produce an individual letter to each member of the church (bearing in mind that every character of every page is individually impressed on the paper). This can also produce heavy printer wear. Moreover, each letter must be hand signed, or the individual effect is lost. In practice, therefore, the facility is only likely to be useful in writing to a much smaller group, such as the members of the church council, and it is doubtful if they will gain much benefit from individual form letters.

In many cases, the best solution is to duplicate or photocopy the letter, and affix an adhesive address label – either to the letter or envelope – for each recipient. The labels are printed using the church membership software without the need to link up with word processing.

The situations where form letters can be useful in churches are where the quantity is not too great, and where, even though the recipients appreciate that the letter is a standard one, they value the element of personalisation. Examples might include follow up letters after weddings or baptisms, invitations to participate in a special working party, or letters to individuals in relation to their financial giving. The advantages are greatest when some personal information such as a date or an amount of money has to be inserted into the body of a letter, which would otherwise have had to be added by hand.

Desk top publishing

Desk top publishing (DTP) represents the ultimate in word processing, whereby the user controls not just the text and layout of the document, but can also select between a number of different typefaces and point sizes in much the same way as a professional printer or publisher might wish to do. DTP packages also give the user full control of page make-up as regards positioning articles on a page, adding headlines, organising columns, and even inserting certain kinds of illustrations.

Good DTP software packages are quite expensive, and they usually require computers with special high resolution screens. Furthermore, although the results can sometimes be produced on a matrix printer, the quality of the different typefaces is easily lost, and DTP really requires a laser printer (see chapter 3).

The cost is not therefore likely to be justified for producing a local church newsletter, and to use DTP effectively requires substantial learning time if the results are to be attractive. However, for churches involved in more advanced publishing activities, DTP may well be worth considering.

Membership and pastoral records

The nature of a church is fundamentally to do with people, and an application to keep track of all the information needed in relation to individual people will come high on the list of priorities in most churches.

At the simplest level, almost all churches need to keep a membership list, an electoral roll list, or a list of parishioners involved in the church. By holding this information on computer, only the changes have to be entered, and a fresh listing can be printed whenever required.

Plenty of software packages exist for keeping lists of names and addresses, but most churches will want their membership system to act as much more than an address list. One needs to keep some indication for each person of the church groups or committees in which they are involved. The membership system can then be used not just for membership lists, but also for lists of those in each housegroup, those in the Sunday school (if children are included), those on the church council, and so on.

The advantage of this approach is that each person's name and address is held just once, and they will appear on every list to which they belong. If the person should move house, or get married, for example, there is only one change to enter, yet next time the various lists come to be printed, the new details about that person will appear everywhere. Similarly, if someone joins the church or moves away, only one entry has to be made.

The idea can be taken a good deal further. For example if, in a stewardship scheme, people are asked to indicate ways they would be able to help in the church, it is a simple matter (with appropriate software) to enter some codes against each name to indicate offers of help with car lifts, property work, catering, teaching, etc. One can then use the membership system to list all those who have offered any particular form of assistance.

It is also useful to keep information on file about each person's approximate age, sex, telephone number, and perhaps some details of occupation or interests. This can allow various directories to be printed, and it is easy to list all those in particular age groups, for example, when new activities are being planned. With this information on file it is also simple to extract statistics such as 'How many members of the church council are under 25?'.

A good membership system will allow considerable choice in the ways of presenting printed listings. There is usually a need for summary listings of names and addresses, for more comprehensive directories with full details about each person, and for the ability to list names and addresses onto labels, for addressing material to individual recipients. Some users may also need the ability to transfer information to a word processing package for production of form letters.

For a church with a good deal happening, this application can be enough to make a computer worthwhile on its own. A membership system is a very effective computer application: for a modest amount of input – putting the names in initially – it is possible to produce a very wide range of outputs in the form of different listings for different purposes.

Names to record

The principle is, of course, not limited just to church *members*. Most churches have a large number of adherents, members of organisations, children, and so on, who must be recorded. Sometimes a community roll for this purpose is already maintained, but if there is no idea of the total, a good rule of thumb in a reasonably active church is to allow a total number of names of around three times the membership.

Churches involved in major work in the community or in evangelistic projects with extensive contacts may need many more names than this. If the software is available it can be used to assist in the care of *all* who are in contact with the church in any way. Some clergy even consider recording all residents of the parish, but except in small rural communities this is not usually viable as there is simply too much information to keep up to date, and there could also be complications under the Data Protection Act (see chapter 7). It is better just to enter names once some contact is made.

For a church with anything over 100 members (or for ministers with over 100 members across several churches in their care) the benefits of a membership system are really quite substantial. For a church with anything over 250 members a great deal of human resources will be wasted if this application is not computerised effectively. But even for a church of 50 members, a membership system can still be useful, particularly where there is significant children's work or work in the community.

One important requirement of a membership system is the ability to handle people both as individuals and as families. The basic information must be held for each individual, otherwise the whole family would appear when listing membership of a group or committee to which one person belongs. But when it comes to printing labels to address newsletters or other circulars, usually only one copy is sent to each family – in fact people can become quite cross at the wastage if they receive several copies of something in one household. Similarly, it is important that once an address is entered for one member of a family, it should not have to be retyped for others.

Pastoral visiting

If suitable software is used, the membership system can be extended into a full vehicle for pastoral care, by assisting in the planning of pastoral visiting.

Typically a visiting frequency is entered for each person. For example, the sick and housebound will perhaps need visits monthly or even weekly, whereas others may only require a six monthly visit or no regular visits at all. When pastoral visits are made the date is entered, and from this the software can determine when the next visit is due. Each week or each month the minister – or others involved in visiting – print a list of forthcoming visits to be made.

Such an approach is much better than a simple computerised diary, because it does not insist that visits have to be made on certain dates; it simply notes when visits are due, and once a visit is made the next one is scheduled accordingly. By entering a yearly frequency it is possible to plan follow up visits on bereavement anniveraries, baptism anniversaries, and so on.

Systems of this kind cannot actually give ministers any more time for visits, but they can help in promoting the most effective pastoral care within the time available.

The principle can also be used for any other regular contact, such as recording dates of attendance at services or meetings. In particular, Presbyterian churches will wish to have facilities of this kind to record attendances at communion.

Church finance

Finance is traditionally an area for use of computers, and although in many churches this may not be the highest priority for computerisation, a computer can still make a very significant contribution to management of church funds. The precise opportunities vary greatly with the size of church; there are a number of possible applications under the general heading of finance.

Bookkeeping and accounts

A computer accounting system allows the user to enter details of all receipts and payments, allocating them to appropriate categories of income and expenditure. From this, the system can produce a range of reports showing transactions under various headings, and in particular, it will print an income and expenditure account and often a balance sheet too. Some systems will also include items such as an automatic comparison with last year.

The main benefit of such a system is in the increased analysis that is possible: the actual effort of entering all the transactions is much the same whether a computer is used or whether this is done manually. But once that information is held on computer, with suitable accounting software it is usually possible to print income and expenditure accounts, and other reports showing up to date figures, almost immediately.

The benefits of such a system are not therefore in the bookkeeping, but in the very great savings of time at end of year, and in the ability to produce up to date reports at any time which may enable the church to make much more effective decisions.

Budgeting

By means of software packages known as *spreadsheets* it is possible to prepare rows and columns of figures with automatic calculation of horizontal and vertical totals, percentage changes, and much more. As soon as one figure is changed the effect on the whole sheet is seen almost immediately.

For those with some financial understanding, a spreadsheet can be an enormously powerful tool for preparing budgets, forecasts, or making decisions about the allocation of money across a number of possible sources or applications (as when deciding how to divide a quota payment or assessment between several churches). A spreadsheet can also be helpful in preparing end of year accounts even when the books themselves are kept manually.

In larger churches where complex financial decisions have to be made, or for any church involved in systematic preparation of budgets, a spreadsheet can be quite a help. If there is a small finance committee they can gain a lot from having the computer in the meeting so that figures are placed on the spreadsheet in response to discussion, enabling immediate consideration of the effect. A wide range of financial 'what if . . .?' questions can be answered effectively in this way.

Deeds of covenant

The reclaiming of income tax on deeds of covenant is an important source of church income, yet administratively the work is substantial, particularly where the local church prepares all the forms for the Inland Revenue claim. On the other hand, if a diocesan or denominational agency is used for this, the church may well be paying a significant percentage to the agency to handle the claim, and much of the detailed control of the process is removed from the local church.

Software packages are now available that allow the full computerisation of deeds of covenant, from recording basic information about each deed and noting monies received, to producing detailed listings, and even quotations for individuals. The software will also produce all the R185 forms, with figures correctly inserted for each covenant, ready to give to covenantors for signature. When these are returned, schedules are printed by computer for the main tax claim document submitted to the authorities.

The advantages of such a system are an enormous saving of time for the covenants secretary – time which can often be better used in other ways in the church. It can also yield greater accuracy leading to less problems and queries, and can enable tax claims to be submitted more promptly. Furthermore, there is also every incentive to obtain as many covenants as possible – even quite small ones – or to ask covenantors regularly to take out new or supplementary covenants, as the additional work involved is minimal once the process is computerised.

Planned giving

The recording of income week by week or month by month under regular giving schemes is quite a chore; this is true whether the income is through envelopes in the church collection or through standing orders. Yet it is often necessary to produce quite detailed reports from this information, either to inform church members of the progress of the giving, or to keep track of income when it relates to a deed of covenant.

One or two software packages are gradually emerging to handle this task. As the envelopes are counted, or as standing orders are checked off from the bank statement, details of reference number and amount are entered immediately onto the computer. From time to time, a contributions statement is printed for each person involved in the scheme, and details are transferred to the accounting system and covenants system if applicable. By requiring different passwords for the various functions used by different officers, the system can maintain total confidentiality between names, numbers, and amounts.

Payroll, stock control, trading

In a very large church which employs several staff (say more than four or five) it may be worth computerising the payroll, so that payslips are produces automatically. Selecting payroll software is a major subject in its own right, as there are many features included in some packages but not others, and it is vital that any software is kept up to date with changes in legislation. The advantages of computerising the payroll become much greater with a larger number of employees; even for the few churches that have five employees (say) the cost of the software and the complexity of getting to grips with it may mean that there is no real benefit in computerisation. However, for those who wish to pursue this possibility there are many payroll packages to choose from.

Stock control is another area, sometimes considered by churches involved in large bookstalls or coffee bars which require extensive stocks. A wide range of stock control software packages are available, but the cost can be quite high, and many are aimed at firms involved in substantial distribution operations so they are frequently much too complex for church work. Stock control packages are often linked in with accounting systems. One has to ask whether manual stock control is sufficient of a problem to justify computerising: the user still has to record everything received into and removed from stock – the package will simply help with the analysis of this.

For churches involved in significant trading activities of this kind or any another there are many additional questions about computing, and it may be necessary to look at software intended for small businesses. Similarly for churches who run schools or conference centres many additional factors must be considered which are outside the scope of this book. In such cases, further advice is definitely required.

Other applications

Apart from the main areas listed above, there is some potential for use of computers in the production of rotas and plans of individual duties and preaching commitments. Unfortunately this is a much more complex area to computerise effectively than is often realised, and a computer program which simply allocates names to slots on a random basis (subject to certain restrictions) is not usually acceptable. The Methodist Circuit Plan is a prime example: several individuals have produced programs which offer some assistance in their own situation, but it is quite another matter to create software of a professional standard that can be used for this kind of application on a widespread basis.

Another area where the computer could offer a good deal once software is available is in the administration of all the occasional offices: baptisms, confirmations, weddings, funerals. A membership system is very useful for keeping the names of those involved, but there is a good deal more that could usefully be done by computer, particularly if it ever becomes acceptable for the statutory registers to be maintained by computer and certificates produced accordingly.

The applications listed above are the main ones concerned with *managing church information*, but there are several other possible uses for computers in the church.

Computers are increasingly found in teaching, and applications suitable for Sunday school work are becoming available. In some cases the quality of the software is rather on the amateur side, but if the demand exists, higher quality packages will undoubtedly emerge. In principle, applications could also be devised for adult teaching work in housegroups, marriage preparation, and so on.

There are also certain computer based aids for theological work. Several packages exist which contain a machine readable copy of the bible, together with various aids for searching and cross referencing. Most of these are American in origin, and are based on the Authorised (King James) Version. In some cases the faciles extend to linking the biblical text with a concordance such as Strong's, allowing identification of the corresponding words in transliterated Greek and Hebrew. There are considerable copyright problems in releasing the bible in this way: the AV is Crown Copyright and the newer translations are the copyright of individual publishers. However, for those involved in biblical study of this kind, such software will clearly be of help. Because of the size of the bible a hard disk computer is almost always needed.

Points for discussion

1. What would be the most appropriate applications to computerise in your church?

2. What would be the main benefits to your church of handling these applications by computer?

3. What other applications can you envisage for church computing, beyond those discussed in this chapter?

4. How does the availability of software affect decisions about the use of computers in the church?

3
Planning and selecting a system ____

Many people have made a great mistake in thinking about computer systems starting from the hardware, and in doing so have frequently bought systems that are next to useless. The problem is that because the hardware is obvious to look at, and because it is frequently the largest part of the cost, it is easy to assume that it forms the first consideration.

How to begin

It will be recalled that computer systems consist of hardware, software, and information.

The right way to start is by considering the information that the church will wish to keep on computer, and even more important, the information that the system must produce. One must ask what the church would wish to do with that information.

This leads to a consideration of the software: What sort of programs will be needed to allow the church to do what is desired with the information? Will that software allow the required information to be entered and stored? Will it then process that information so that it can be selected and printed out in the manner needed?

Having found some suitable software, only then is hardware seriously considered. For it is an important restriction that most software will only run on a few types of computer, so that selecting the hardware first frequently leads to the problem of finding no suitable software available.

The fundamental rule in selecting a system is to start by considering the information to be processed – the reason for wanting a system in the first place – and with that in mind, *choose the software, then the hardware.*

The remainder of this chapter offers an approach for this process of selection.

Changes in technology

Because of the rapidly changing nature of products in the computer field and the frequent price changes, we make no attempt to recommend *specific* products – either hardware or software – for church use. However, it is possible to define the *criteria* that should be used in selecting church systems.

This rapid change does mean that one cannot spend too long making a decision: if one spends a year looking at a number of different products, it is likely that by the end of that time, the products considered initially will have acquired important new features, or may be priced very differently, or may have been withdrawn from the market.

Once it is clear therefore that a system is likely to be purchased, it is necessary to work to a fairly tight timescale – perhaps three months at the outside – in which to consider the products available, make a decision, and place orders with the relevant suppliers.

Until that point is reached it is, of course, worth collecting literature about possible products for future consideration, but there is probably little to be gained from spending time with demonstrations, unless this is needed purely to appreciate the possibilities of church computing. When a purchase is becoming more likely it is then vital to contact suppliers for current prices and specifications, and to ascertain the precise suitability of different products.

The rapid changes in computer technology can be difficult to appreciate, and there is sometimes a danger of thinking continually that by delaying the purchase it would be possible to obtain a system for a substantially lower price.

However, there are several problems with this argument.

The first is that whilst there is a long term trend towards increasing power and sophistication coupled with decreasing prices, it is usually only when new products are launched that significant price changes occur. Once a product (hardware or software) becomes available, it is unusual for there to be any significant price reduction until it is almost obsolete and about to be replaced. Rather, it is quite common for the price of successful products to be *increased* one they are established.

The second point is that the system will consist of several products: computer, printer, several software packages, initial supplies, and a price change in one of these items may not make a vast difference to the cost of the whole system.

Thirdly, much time can be wasted by hoping for products which have been announced but are not yet available (the term 'vapour-ware' has been used to describe such items!). Very often these products are launched later than planned, cost more than planned, or sometimes fail to reach the market at all. Even when they are released, there are often serious shortages, if the product is popular, and there may be reliability problems.

Whilst the prospect of future enhancements may be used to swing the balance between two alternative systems that otherwise seem equally suitable, a church would be taking a very dangerous risk to make a decision – or delay the purchase of an alternative – on the basis of a possible order for products not yet released.

But the fourth and most important point is that delaying may not leave the church any better off. If it is established that a computer system will offer benefits for the church, then the longer it is delayed, the longer it is before those benefits begin to be seen. It may be that the loss of those benefits (whether financial or spiritual) due to a six month delay, for example, could be much more significant than any possible price saving.

So, once it is established that a computer system will be of benefit to a church, sufficient to justify the cost as measured on current prices, one should proceed as soon as possible to select and order a suitable collection of products.

Choosing the software

Once it is clear how information is to be used, a number of applications will have been identified from those listed in the previous chapter. It is then necessary to consider the choice of software for each of these. But first, there are some general principles to consider.

Packages or one-off developments?

There are two possible approaches for software: one can either buy a ready made software package or one can arrange to have software written on a one-off basis to one's own requirements.

A software package consists of programs that have been written and tested by an independent software house, together with appropriate documentation (manuals etc).

For churches, there are many advantages in using packages, and this approach should be followed as far as possible.

In the first place, the package approach is usually much cheaper. The extensive development costs of the software are shared between all those who purchase it. As a result, if the software package has been professionally developed, one is usually obtaining a much better product than could ever be commissioned on a one-off basis.

A second reason is that software packages are usually fairly well proven. There will often be other churches or organisations who have used the package and established its worth. Most of the faults will be eliminated.

A third important reason is that software packages are usually available immediately. If software is developed on a one-off basis it may be months or even years before it is available.

Fourthly, it is very difficult for an inexperienced computer user to specify accurately what would be their requirements for a one-off development, and frequently the software fails to achieve much of what was originally anticipated.

Fifthly, good software packages are provided with very comprehensive manuals to guide the user. It is usually impossible with a one-off development to produce more than the briefest of documentation; often there is none at all.

Sometimes people feel even despite these factors, that it may be worth writing software on a one-off basis if it can be done free of charge, either by the user or by someone else in the church.

Nothing could be further from the truth! Even if this expertise is available – whether from a professional or an amateur programmer – it is a colossal task to write software to the same standard of reliability, flexibility, and error handling, that will be found in good quality software packages. Almost always this will be the wrong stewardship of the individual's time even if offered freely: there must be more important contributions that such a person could make in church life with the time available.

But there are even more serious difficulties in terms of ongoing support when software is 'home-written'. What if problems are found, or if requirements change? What if the person who wrote the program moves away or no longer has the time available?

The dangers of using locally written software are immense, and if computers are to be used effectively as a matter of church strategy, it is infinitely preferable to restrict the consideration to professionally produced software packages.

The only case where a one-off development may be justified is in a large church with a very important application that is virtually unique, and for which no suitable software package is available. It may then be worth commissioning software specifically for that requirement, provided a firm is used that understands the application, and has experience of developments on the hardware required. The costs will be quite high (usually higher than the hardware cost unless the application is very simple) and the application must be very important to justify it. Most churches that have initially considered developments of this kind have tended to opt out after a specification is prepared with detailed costs. But in certain cases – particularly if there is a possibility of sharing the cost with a few others needing the same application – this approach may be justifiable.

In other cases, small software houses may be prepared to modify their packages for specific clients, and this may be appropriate if there is a package which meets many but not all of the requirements for a particular application.

The remainder of this section assumes that the church system will be based on packaged software.

Start with the most unusual application

It may seem logical to start software selection with the application that seems to be most common, but this is in fact the wrong approach. One might temporarily ignore applications which the church would not mind leaving unautomated, but of those applications which are considered virtually essential, it is important to start with the most unusual or the most complex.

For example, if the main applications are to be day to day word processing and deeds of covenant, one should start by considering software for covenants, as this is a far more specific requirement, even though the word processing application may be used much more frequently.

Word processing packages are available for virtually all machines, but there are not likely to be many software packages designed for managing deeds of covenant, so the covenants package that is selected will have to determine the choice of hardware.

Once the choice of hardware has been narrowed down by this consideration, it may be that all the remaining software will have to be selected with the requirement that it must run on the defined hardware, unless the church is considering a number of totally unrelated applications and is prepared to consider several different machines. In general, a mixture of hardware leads to operational difficulties, but where a church wishes, for example, to use computers both for educational games in the Sunday school and for administrative applications in the church office, then it is really much better to have quite separate hardware for each aspect.

Matched or mixed?

Where a number of applications are considered, much can be gained if the software for each is produced by the same developer.

For example, if a membership software package is obtained from one source, an accounting package from another source, and a package for recording envelopes from a third source, these packages may all work individually, but they may have little in common.

The three packages are likely to have different kinds of screen layouts, different commands to use them, different ways of entering data, and different formats of printed reports. This will be very confusing to those who have to use the system, and may make it very difficult to produce consistent information for decision making.

Most professional software developers adopt a common standard for the user interface across all their packages in a given range, so if there are two suppliers both offering a number of packages of interest, it is preferable to buy all from one or all from the other.

Moreover, as requirements become more complex, it is increasingly necessary for different software packages to link up, in order to transfer the information processed by one to another. For example, it is only possible to produce individually addressed letters to church members using a word processing package, if their names and addresses can be obtained from the membership package (unless the user is prepared to re-enter addresses in the form needed for the word processing). Similarly, the use of the deed of convenant system may need members' addresses to be obained from a membership system. Or an envelope system may need to transfer amounts received to an accounting system.

Most software developers are gradually moving towards *integrated* software whereby several different applications are able to transfer information from one to another. In some cases, all the software is marketed as a single product, with modules for different applications.

It is thus wise to select a software supplier who is likely to be able to meet most of the applications the church will need both immediately and in the longer term. Even if the supplier cannot offer all the software themselves, at least by following their recommendations for other applications one is following a safer path than selecting at random from many software suppliers.

Church specific or general purpose software?

A few of the applications being considered will be amenable to general purpose software; other applications will require software developed specifically for church work.

This distinction is crucial. An application such as word processing is not specific to church work; almost all users of personal computers are likely to require the ability to edit and print letters, documents, reports, and so on. Word processing software can thus be selected from the variety of popular packages available (though if there is a requirement to link with other software for production of form letters, the choice may be limited by this requirement). On the other hand, if facilities are needed for word processing in Greek and Hebrew, in order to write theological papers, the word processing requirement becomes much more church specific, and specialised hardware is likely to be needed, too. In such cases it is vital to consult a firm with appropriate specialist expertise.

Similarly, spreadsheet packages for financial planning are a general purpose application that will interest many computer users. The only constraints of choice are likely to be if information must be transferred from an accounting package to a spreadsheet.

On the other hand, the administration of charitable deeds of covenant is highly specialised, and software for this purpose would only be used by churches and charities. Because of the complex forms which the software has to issue, and the need to conform to Inland Revenue requirements, it is virtually impossible to computerise covenants without church specific software.

Likewise, the management of envelope systems for regular giving, with the production of suitable reports, is not an application that is easily handled without software written for the job, and few would attempt to do so.

However, for some other applications, it is harder for the inexperienced user to choose between church specific software and more general purpose packages, and guidelines are useful.

The most important such area is church membership – frequently the key application for a church computer system. There are many general purpose 'database' software packages available which allow one to set up computerised record cards of names, addresses, and similar information, and at first one might assume such packages would be suitable for church membership applications.

If that is *all* that a church is seeking from a membership system, a database package may be adequate. But in most cases there will be additional important functions of a church specific nature. For example, in church work it is important to be able to communicate both with individuals and with families. Most database packages (apart from the most complex which would be beyond the ability of most church users to set up themselves) require that each 'record card' is a single entity – either an individual, or a family. If the records are kept by individual, one cannot produce labels to address newsletters for one copy per family; rather every individual would have to receive a newsletter. Conversely, if records are kept as families, it is impossible to list the members of the church council, since whole families would appear.

If the membership system is also to be used as a basis for pastoral visiting or outreach work, then the application is even more specific, and software will have to be chosen with provision for planning of visiting. It is most unlikely this could be achieved in a database package without great complexity.

Moreover, database packages, by virtue of their flexibility to keep records for many different purposes, need extensive initial work in defining the types of information and how it is to be accessed. Church specific software is likely to be designed around church needs, and will thus usually need much less initial configuration. Only if a church has some very complex requirement which the church packages cannot handle is there likely to be any advantage in using general purpose databases, and even then, the greater flexibility must be weighed against all the disadvantages cited.

Another application where there may be a choice between church specific and general purpose packages is in the accounting area. There are vast numbers of software packages produced for accounting, mostly aimed primarily at the small business, and although quite a few church treasurers have managed to apply these in church work, there are a number of snags to overcome.

Unfortunately, at the very cheapest end, many of the pure cashbook packages have tended to be very limited in scope, and rather unsatisfactory in terms of maintaining an effective audit trail to allow all transactions to be traced and verified. The next level of accounting packages tend to be based strongly around the concept of sales and purchase ledgers, which can be cumbersome. Few churches receive enough invoices from suppliers for purchases of goods and services to justify a purchase ledger, and unless a church is raising numerous invoices for hall lettings (for example) a sales ledger is even less useful: it can seem very inappropriate to have to record collections and donations as though they were 'sales'. Similarly, most small business packages place great emphasis on the handling of value added tax which is very frustrating for churches, where VAT is not separated.

Therefore, if suitable church-specific accounting software is available, it offers a number of advantages in approach. It is likely to be much easier for most treasurers to use, and will probably produce printed reports in a form suited for church needs, rather than using headings like 'sales', 'profit before tax' and so on.

A further important advantage of church specific software is in the documentation. It is much easier to use software with manuals which assume that the user will be in a church, deal with the information in a church oriented way, and use church examples, than to use a package aimed largely at small businesses, where the user continually has to translate the issues in the manual to the usage in church work.

The price of software packages is very much related to the likely number of purchasers, simply because the development costs, advertising costs, and so on can be shared between more customers. A simple word processing package that is likely to sell tens of thousands of copies will normally cost much less than a highly specialised application such as deeds of covenant for which the developers will do very well if they sell a hundred copies. So in principle, church specific software packages would normally cost more than comparable general purpose packages. However, at the time of writing, the main firms producing church specific packages deliberately charge subsidised prices for church applications, so in practice the additional costs may be minimal or non-existent, and certainly the advantages of church specific packages are normally very significant.

Assessing software suitability

Church specific software is naturally a specialised area, and in the foreseeable future there will be only a limited number of software houses choosing to develop for the church field. For many applications, the critera above will lead to only one software package that can be seriously considered. But even if that is the case, its suitability must still be carefully assessed.

If there is more than one possible package or range of packages to consider for a given application, churches need to be able to weigh their suitability, and make a decision.

The following questions might be considered in evaluating a software package:

- will it enable us to record the information we require?

- will it enable us to produce the information we require as output? Does it have the facility to produce the listings we need? Can we enquire on the information held in the ways we need?

- is the software clear and straightforward to use?

- is it provided with good documentation that will enable us to use it well? Is the documentation understandable to those who will have to use it?

- what kind of support can be expected from the supplier, both in assisting with queries and in rectifying any faults that may be found?

- is it an established package with a number of existing users? Is it proved in other churches – or are other users mainly commercial?

- once the software is received, will we simply be left to it unless we complain – or is there a user group or newsletter to keep us in touch?

- if we are likely to need services such as training or individual modifications, are these available? Are there other packages from the same supplier which may be of use in the future?

Software evaluation is a subject that could occupy a whole book. It is important to appreciate that if you are considering a package, it will have been developed to meet the needs of a broad range of users, and as such it will never do everything 100 per cent as one would wish. It is always worth seeing if you can alter your own procedures slightly to fit in with the approach taken by a given package.

Similarly a church may have to balance the advantages of special features that are only available in a new, rather unproven package, against the benefits of using a more established package that may lack one or two 'bells and whistles'. But never compromise on documentation and support unless there is no alternative; it is very difficult to make a really dependable church tool out of a system that is based on uncertain software.

Software licensing

When software is sold, the user does not actually own the programs that make up the package. Instead, what one is actually buying is a *licence to use the software on a given machine.*

The user will normally become owner of the diskettes and manual that are supplied when the package is ordered. But although the diskettes contain a copy of the programs, the programs themselves are owned by the software developer. Copyright of the software remains with the developer, and the user can only take copies of the programs under strictly defined conditions.

For specialist software, you may well be required to sign a software licence agreement before the software is supplied. This will state the terms on which the software is provided (including details of any guarantee) and the ways in which it can be used. For other packages, you may find the licence printed on the package as you receive it, with an indication that if you open the package or proceed to use it, then you are deemed to have accepted the licence conditions.

The authors of computer software enjoy copyright protection in the same way as the author of a book, and copies can only be made with the author's (or publisher's) permission. Loading and running a program involves it being copied from diskette into the computer memory, so this can only be done with permission of the copyright holder. The software licence will indicate the conditions behind this.

Most software licences allow the user to run the program on one machine (sometimes you even have to given the serial number of your computer, and inform the developers if you change machines). Generally speaking, a second copy of the software must be purchased if a second machine is used – although smaller software houses will often allow a discount on second copies.

In a few cases, the licence will allow use of the software on any one computer at a time (so a minister who has a machine in the church office and a machine in the vicarage could run the software on either one at a time, but would be breaking the licence if a secretary used the software on one machine and the minister used it on the other at the same time).

Other licences are occasionally issued in the name of a given user, such as a particular church. This sometimes called a corporate licence or a site licence, and governs the use of all computers owned by a given organisation or used at a given address. In such cases, the user can freely purchase additional machines, but must take care to ensure that the software is not used for the activities of any organisation not covered by the licence.

Where a number of churches wish to use a given package it may be worth approaching the developers to ask if they would be prepared to agree to a corporate licence to cover all churches in a given diocese or even in a whole denomination. It is often possible to obtain substantial discounts compared to many churches purchasing individually. However, suppliers will not usually agree to such arrangements unless they can be confident that copies of the software will be strictly controlled and only used in the organisation covered by the licence.

Software copyright is a sensitive issue, and since the Copyright (Computer Software) Amendment Act 1985 it is possible for those making illegal copies of computer software to face very large fines and up to two years imprisonment.

It is normally so easy to make a copy of some software – simply by copying the diskette – that developers insist on strict licensing. Software packages can only be made available at a reasonable price if all those who use a given package pay a licence fee and contribute to the development costs.

Because of the problem of illegal copies, some suppliers produce software in a copy protected form, whereby the program diskette is modified in such a way that it cannot be copied. This is inconvenient for the user, as backup copies of the software cannot be made to guard against disk failure. It is to be hoped that all computer users will exercise honesty and avoid the need for copy protected software.

In churches, there is rarely a problem of deliberate software theft, but users can sometimes be in breach of a software licence through ignorance (particularly when second machines are bought). In other areas such as schools, so much illegal copying has taken place that few suppliers are prepared to produce software for that field. When purchasing software for church work, one needs to be aware of the terms of the licence, and train all users of the system to appreciate the requirements that the licence imposes.

A user who is found to be in breach of a software licence will at the very least find their right to use the software withdrawn, and in more serious cases, may well end up in court.

Choosing the hardware

Once the software is chosen, the choice of hardware will be limited to machines that support that software. Nevertheless, this may still leave quite a choice, particularly where the software will run on any of a number of different computers in a range.

At the time of writing there is a tendency for most hardware and software suppliers to move towards the standard established by the IBM Personal Computer (IBM PC), and a great many machines are sold as being 'IBM PC compatible' – that is, they will run software that is written for the IBM PC. Software developers are moving in a similar direction, as by developing software to the IBM PC standard it will run on all other machines compatible with that.

This gives the user quite a wide choice; there are presently at least 50 suppliers producing computers that are IBM PC compatible, and most of these have several machines in their range. As systems develop, new standards will emerge, but the user still has to select suitable hardware within the range of machines that will run the chosen software.

The hardware is usually purchased as two main components: the computer itself and the printer. In some cases these are supplied together, but usually the user can decide on the computer and printer separately.

The computer

Having established that the computer will run the chosen software, the next most important requirement is the capacity of its disk drives, as this will determine how much information can be stored.

The disks are used to hold both the programs to be run, and the information for the user. For example, if the computer is to be used for word processing, disks must be used both for the word processing software, and for storing documents that the user wishes to edit. Depending on the system, one disk drive may be used for both purposes, or one disk may be used for programs and another for data.

A computer with a floppy disk drive (left) *and hard disk* (right). *The hard disk is totally enclosed, and only a small light indicates when it is used.*

Capacity for storing information is measured in *bytes*; a byte is the space required to hold one character – one letter or digit. For significant amounts of data, the term *kilobyte* (kb or just K) is used for about a thousand bytes, and *megabyte* (Mb) for around a million bytes.

To give a feel for this, a typed page of A4 text typically has 60 lines each with about 70 characters across the line, so it needs about 4200 bytes (or roughly 4 K) to store a page of data – perhaps a little less as not all lines will be the full length. The New Testament is about a million bytes long (1 Mb).

Disk drives work magnetically so that information can be retained for long term use when the computer is switched off. There are two main approaches.

A *floppy disk drive* will record or read information on a *diskette*. Different diskettes can be inserted into the drive at different times. The capacity of the disk drive determines how much information can be recorded on any one diskette. Diskettes are very convenient when information has to be transferred away from the machine. Software is usually supplied on diskette, and diskettes are often used as the means of taking backup copies of information held on a hard disk. All machines thus need at least one floppy disk drive. On the IBM PC standard, a floppy diskette can hold 360 K, perhaps enough for membership records of a thousand people, depending on the software used. Other machines have floppy disks of substantially higher capacity.

A *hard disk* (or a Winchester disk – named after the place of its invention) is permanently held within its drive. The disk and the drive are essentially one and the same. Because of this, the whole assembly is sealed and dust free, so the disk can rotate much faster and information can be recorded much more densely. A hard disk thus offers the capacity to store much more information than a floppy drive – 20 Mb is a popular size – and for a church needing large membership files or complex software this may be a big advantage. Access to information may also be rather more rapid. On the other hand, it can be more complex to set up hard disk systems initially, and taking backup copies of information can be more complex.

At the time of writing, costs are such that smaller churches will normally use machines with two floppy disk drives and larger churches are tending to opt for hard disk systems. However, as manufacturers launch new machines the price balance will change.

In considering the capacity to store information, what is *not* important is the amount of internal electronic memory (sometimes called RAM). It can sound very impressive in advertisements when one machine has more RAM than another, but it does not affect the amount of information that can be stored on disk. More RAM may allow the user to run more complex programs, but provided a machine has sufficient memory for the proposed software, there is normally no benefit in having any more.

Other factors to consider in choosing between different computers that will all run the software required are the quality of the screen and keyboard, and the overall robustness.

One of the ways in which manufacturers of inexpensive machines keep costs down is by using cheaper screens and keyboards, and by designing generally on a less rugged basis. For many church users – particularly individual ministers – it is unlikely that the machine will be subject to very heavy use, and it is often worth accepting these limitations for a substantially lower cost. But where the machine may be used for eight hours a day in a church office, or where it will have to be carried around between more than one location, quality of design can become important.

The characters on a high quality screen will be considerably sharper and easier to work with for long periods. A monochrome monitor is preferable to a colour one for most church applications, as the characters are usually sharper, and it is also likely to be cheaper. It is only for elaborate graphics and for games that colour monitors offer any real advantage.

Similarly, a good quality keyboard can often be helpful, particularly where the user is a skilled typist. Cheap keyboards can also prove their limitation if the users are a number of heavy fisted individuals; sooner or later one key will fail, which is more frustrating than a total breakdown! A metal rather than plastic casing is also of value if the machine is likely to get a bashing.

Finally, there can be differences between two otherwise identical computers in the processor speed, that is the speed at which the computer processes the instructions that make up the programs. This is a rather technical area: processor speeds on microcomputers are measured in megahertz (MHz). A standard IBM PC works at 4.77 MHz whereas many compatibles work at 8 MHz – this means that the programs run nearly twice as fast. This is further complicated by the type of processor: an 80286 processor is considerably faster and more powerful than an 8086, for example.

In practice this difference is not as important as it seems, because the speed of most programs is limited by the disks, the printer, or by the speed at which the user can enter data. However, a faster processor can make certain functions a bit quicker as when using a word processing package to search for a given word in a long document.

The printer

The choice of printer is largely dictated by two main criteria: speed and quality. For most church applications, the quality of what the computer prints onto paper is of considerable importance, and is a major factor in the choice of system. Speed is often perceived as being of less importance, but whilst a very slow printer may be acceptable for printing the final version of a letter, it can be very frustrating if it takes half an hour to print just a draft of a six page report or a membership listing in a large church.

However, none of these factors must be allowed to override the criteria about choice of software. The best printer in the world is of no use if the software fails to allow the user to produce the printed information required.

The speed of a printer is usually measured in characters per second (cps) – the number of printed characters (letters, digits, etc) that can be printed in one second. Bearing in mind that a full page of A4 text will have about 4000 characters, it follows that the time taken to print each page at various speeds would be as shown in the table.

Printer speed	Time to print a page of 4000 characters
15 cps	4 min 26 s
50 cps	1 min 20 s
120 cps	30 s
300 cps	13 s

In practice these times will be slightly longer, to allow for the line feeding as the printer moves down the page. When considering print times, it is worth noting that a memberhip listing in a medium to large church, or a batch of form letters, may well require 20 pages, depending on the amount of detail included in each case.

Choosing a printer that is too slow can greatly reduce the effectiveness of the computer system. On the other hand, a smaller church or individual minister may well be able to manage with a much slower printer than a busy church office.

As regards the printed result, there are several methods of producing a printed image onto paper. Some of the results are shown on the next page.

The most popular method at present is the *dot matrix* printer which works by means of needles behind a ribbon producing dots on the page to form the shape of the characters. Some people are put off by having seen examples of very poor matrix printing, and assume that all matrix printers are the same. The great advantage of the matrix printer is that because of the dot principle, it is possible for an enormous variety of different kinds of print to be produced: for

Drafting quality — This is a rapid print for ordinary computer printouts such as membership lists and financial data, or for drafts of documents being word processed.

Emphasised Quality — For documents of wider circulation, such as study guides, reports, memos, etc, this emphasised quality print is very attractive.

Near Letter Quality - the face which looks more like a conventional typewriter. Use it for letters and other external material.

This is another NLQ typeface which does not attempt to look like a typewriter, but provides a *very clear* readable print. This is printed at 10 characters per inch (cpi).

Where space is tighter, printing at 12 cpi is useful.

A very small condensed print is useful for financial reports: £123,456.78

Enlarged Headings Too!

Many of the print modes can even be **double printed** or *italicised* to highlight certain words, and one can also use subscripts e.g H_2O or superscripts[5,6] for footnotes.

- *Matrix printer (Epson EX800–9 pin)*

SUSAN BLOGGS	11 The Walk
JOANNA JENKINS	39 St Peter's Parade
JAMES SWITHIN	23 Hill Road

- *Daisywheel printer (Juki 6100)*

The Canon Laser prints at 8 pages per minute 500 characters per second.

The LBP-8A1 makes crisp, clear printouts in black, a more unconventional brown, and comes with four typef

- *Laser printer (Canon LBP–8A1)*

Samples of print from various types of printer.

example matrix printers usually allow one to change from upright to italic characters in the middle of some text, they generally support more than one size of character, they allow material to be emboldened, and (given suitable software) they can even produce graphs and illustrations. Some will offer these forms in more than one typeface.

Most matrix printers support several different qualities of print for different purposes. The draft print is the fastest – usually at least 100 cps, sometimes 300 cps or higher, through it is obviously a little 'dotty'. Many then offer a memo quality or emphasised quality, in which dots are placed between the previous dots to offer a much smoother and blacker impression, convenient for reports, minutes, etc; this is typically at about half of the draft speed. The best quality is called near letter quality (NLQ) or correspondence quality, and involves the printer head making more than one pass over the paper to create the full shape of each character. The result of this is very similar to the type of characters printed by a typewriter, and if a good ribbon is used it is often hard for the casual observer to tell the difference. The speed of NLQ printing is usually much slower – 15 to 50 cps being common – but with a matrix printer one has the flexibility to use draft or NLQ as required for different purposes.

The very highest quality matrix printers use more dot pins to create each character: 24 pins one above the other being common instead of the usual nine. Only a few churches are likely to need this quality, but those who would be printing large amounts of NLQ text may find a 24 pin printer worthwhile. With good paper and a new ribbon the quality from such printers can be outstanding, and the NLQ print speed is usually rather higher than in a nine pin printer.

Until recently, the main alternative to matrix printers has been the *daisywheel* printer which works exactly as a daisywheel electric typewriter, but under computer control. Each character is formed by the shape impressed by the daisywheel through the ribbon. By inserting different daisywheels, different typefaces can be used, but it is not usually viable to change into italics (say) part way through a document.

If the object is to create the greatest possible similarity to electric typing, the daisywheel is the ideal approach, as it works the same way. However, few churches are primarily concerned to deceive the outside world into thinking that they are not using a computer when in fact they are! The speed of most daisywheels is quite a limitation – anything above 25 cps is very expensive – and this can seriously limit the use of the computer for draft printouts.

Another factor with daisywheels is the type of ribbon. For high quality electric typing most typists use a carbon film ribbon, and these can be used in daisywheel printers. But because a computer can produce as much print in a day as the average typist will produce in a couple of months, the cost of using film ribbons in a daisywheel printer can be prohibitive, and most daisywheel users prefer a reusable fabric ribbon, though the results of this are rarely better than with an NLQ matrix printer.

It is possible to purchase a computer interface for certain kinds of electronic typewriter, so that they can be used as a computer printer (one should consult the typewriter supplier to pursue this). However, the cost is often quite high, and the speed is usually only around 15 cps, as that is the most that is needed for typing. Moreover, it can be very inconvenient to have one's typewriter tied up for long periods in this way. The use of a typewriter attachment may be useful for a second printer for special purposes, but if used as the only printer it is most unlikely an effective church system will result.

Both matrix and daisywheel printers tend to generate considerable noise, which can be a problem if others are working in the same room. It is possible to buy accoustic hoods, but they are quite complex devices with extensive padding and cooling fans, and the cost can be nearly as much as the printer itself. The remaining approaches, though considerably more expensive, seek to overcome this.

The *ink jet* printer works by squirting tiny drops of ink on to a page in order to create the characters. The better ink jet printers offer very good quality and very high speed, but costs are currently higher than most churches are able to consider.

The *thermal ink transfer* approach was developed by IBM for their patented Quietwriter. It uses a ribbon, but the ink is gently melted on to the page, rather than transferred by impact. Quality and speed are similar to a daisywheel printer, but with costs rather higher. The speed and cost of ribbons tend, however, to be a limiting factor in drafting.

The other method, which is growing in popularity, is the *laser* printer. Laser printers work on a similar principle to plain paper photocopiers, but instead of copying a printed original, the image to be printed is formed on the drum by a laser beam under computer control. The cost of laser printers is several times higher than matrix and daisywheel printers, and supplies are usually charged at so much per page printed, similar to a copier. The advantage is that a very high quality print is possible in a vast range of type faces and sizes. A good laser printer gives a quality as good as a photocopier produces from the very best originals (though not, of course, as good as true typesetting on a phototypesetter). The speed of laser printers is usually measured in pages per minute (ppm) regardless of the number of characters on the page, but for comparison, a laser printer working at 6 ppm would be equivalent to 400 cps, using our example of 4000 characters on a page. Laser printers are mainly used in conjunction with desk top publishing as an application (see chapter 2); it would be out of proportion to invest in a laser printer for ordinary administrative applications.

It is worth noting that only those printers that work by impact, that is matrix and daisywheel, can be used to produce carbon copies or to cut stencils. If it is an important requirement to be able to produce computer output on to duplicating stencils, a daisywheel will usually give the better result. But if access is available to an electronic stencil scanner, it is possible to use any kind of printer to produce a printed image on paper, and use a scanner to produce a stencil.

In this context one should consider that word processing offers only limited benefits with single page documents such as church notice sheets, and if one needs to squeeze a lot of information into a restricted space by using half line spacing between paragraphs for example, the manual control offered by a typewriter is often worth more than the editing facilities of word processing. It would therefore be unwise to make the ability to cut stencils a prime requirement if this was the only frequent application that required it.

If there are likely to be a few occasions when very high quality is required – perhaps to produce original artwork for outside commercial printing – it may be worth using the services of a computer typesetter, rather than investing in a very expensive printer that would only really be needed occasionally. A number of typesetting firms are now able to receive material on diskette and typeset directly from that, which means one can use ordinary word processing software to prepare the text.

Most printers are available in two *widths*: the standard 80 column type and a wider one that will print 132 columns. In general there is little benefit for church applications in having more than 80 columns; the main use for wider printers is in accounting systems that print large statements or schedules. A wider printer can be attractive for use with spreadsheet applications, but most 80 column printers can produce a condensed print that allows at least 132 characters within the standard width, and for the occasional financial planning job this is normally quite acceptable.

There is also a choice in methods of stationery handling. Nearly all printers offer *friction feed* which allows the user to insert individual sheets of paper (letterheads, for example). However, this is inconvenient for longer reports and listings, which are normally produced on continuous stationery with sprocket holes at the side – with most software other than word processing this is compulsory. (It is best to buy the sort in which the sprocket holes are perforated and can be torn off for a less computer-like appearance and more convenient size.) To feed continuous stationery accurately needs a *tractor feed*; this is included in most printers, but with some it is an optional extra. If large amounts of material will be printed on single sheets, for example form letters to be printed on individual letterheads, a *single sheet feeder* is really required to take a stack of sheets and feed them one by one into the printer. A single sheet feeder does, however, add significantly to the cost, and it can require a good deal of skill with the word processing package to use a sheet feeder correctly, so it is generally a good idea to avoid purchasing sheet feeders until they are clearly needed.

As with the computer itself, it is also common with printers to find several makes offering virtually identical functions at different prices, though the price differences are not usually as wide as the computer. Again, one pays a little more for a name with proven reliability, and a more robust construction. Since the printer is the most mechanical part of the system, and thus potentially the most prone to breakdown, it is unwise to go for the cheapest possible approach.

It is also worth stressing that the most expensive printers can produce very poor results if ribbons (or supply cartridges in ink jet and laser printers) are used for too long. To get a consistently good result, a church must be willing to budget for a reasonable supply of spare ribbons.

Printers and software

The need to ensure software and hardware will work together is just as important for the printer as for the computer. For example, the mere fact that a printer supports italics, underlining, and different typefaces is of little benefit unless one's software has the ability to control those features on the printer chosen. Without that ability, the software will still produce printed documents, and possibly by setting switches on the printer it might be possible to produce a whole document in bold print, for example. But to exercise changes of print style within a document, the software must be programmed to send the necessary controls to the printer at the right point, and the exact controls involved can vary from one printer to another.

This is unlikely to matter in an accounts package, for example, where a listing of transactions in the standard typeface is all that is needed. But with a word processing package, the ability to control the printer at this level is most important, and in choosing a printer it is vital to ensure that it will be supported by the chosen word processing package. Even for an application such a membership listing, it is much more attractive if the software can control the printer to produce underlined headings, for example.

Fortunately, this problem is getting easier, and most printers now tend to conform to one of the popular standards, such as the Epson standard for matrix printers or the Diabolo standard for daisywheels, and if the software offers support for the chosen standard, it should work with any conforming printer.

Even so, few word processing packages allow the user direct control of more obscure changes of format that a printer might allow (e.g. changing the print quality or line spacing within a document) and instead one has to use special word processing commands to send the actual control code to the printer. Whilst some users find this fascinating, for most this requires technical understanding beyond what they find of interest, so one needs to avoid unrealistic assumptions about the complexity of documents that it may be possible to produce.

Suppliers and support

One of the major considerations in choosing a system is where to buy it. There are quite a number of options depending on the service required, and on the software involved.

The choice of system begins with the software, so once this is decided, particularly for specialised applications, it will normally be clear who will supply it. For church specific packages, the software will usually be provided by the software house that developed it (although some software houses are increasingly appointing local agents, so it may be possible to purchase the software through a local dealer).

General purpose software may also be offered by a specialist software house, but if not, it is easiest to buy software such as word processing packages and spreadsheets from the hardware supplier.

For the hardware, there are several options. Some software houses will supply a complete system: hardware and software together (sometimes called a 'turnkey' system, because one should simply be able to turn the key – or switch on – and run the chosen applications). This is certainly advantageous in terms of support, as one is dealing with a single supplier for the whole system, so if queries arise one always turns to the same place. If the software house offers to supply the hardware, this option should not be rejected without good reason, even if other suppliers may be able to offer the hardware a little cheaper. This is particularly beneficial if the system is being purchased with an initial day's training, as the supplier can deliver the system, set it up, and show the user how the hardware and software are used, all at the same time.

However, the advantages of having a single supplier can be outweighed by other factors. Few specialist software houses have their own hardware maintenance engineers – and even if they do, they certainly cannot cover the whole country – so the hardware maintenance will normally be arranged through the hardware manufacturer or an independent maintenance firm. Thus it is not really true that all problems will be dealt with by the same firm, as if a problem is clearly due to hardware, it has to be pursued with the relevant engineers.

Moreover, if hardware faults arise there is a distinct advantage in dealing with a local firm. There is no great problem in using a software supplier who is some way away, because diskettes can easily be sent through the post, but if hardware problems emerge, particularly in the early days, then with a local supplier it is sometimes possible to take the machine back and exchange it.

In terms of local suppliers there are two main options: the computer dealers and the high street multiples.

The high street multiple electronics chains only stock the most popular machines, and they are geared to selling boxes rather than providing a service of dealing with complex questions. However, their prices can be attractive, and because of their size they are unlikely to disappear next week. For serious equipment they can sometimes offer attractively priced repair schemes.

Computer dealers vary greatly in the service they provide. Like car dealers, they usually only sell machines for a limited number of manufacturers. In many cases they have to sell certain numbers of machines so their advice is rarely impartial. Maintaining profitability is dependent on sales, and both large and small dealers cease trading with horrifying frequency. Their staff are sometimes poorly trained, and are often inclined to bluff rather than admit ignorance. Usually they will only be familiar with a limited number of software packages, and may press users towards those. Whatever they say about support, some dealers offer very little help after purchase unless one is buying substantial additional equipment. Moreover, particularly in large cities, dealer sales staff move around very rapidly, and the support may fall remarkably after the salesperson one was dealing with has left.

However, the better local dealers will spare no efforts to offer assistance to clients before and after purchase, and if they have their own maintenance staff (preferably more than one, in case of sickness etc) they can be the best hardware suppliers of all. The only guarantee is personal recommendation from someone with long experience of the firm's service.

If specialist software is being purchased, it is usually best to look to the software house for any assistance in that area. One cannot expect a dealer to get involved in the details of a church specific application that they are unlikely to encounter again.

For the very cheapest hardware, there are certain firms who are pure 'box shippers', supplying hardware essentially on a mail order basis, mainly from magazine advertisements. In general, they offer no support at all, and this approach should only be considered by those with existing computer experience, or if the whole operation is being overseen by a consultant who will provide all assistance required. However, several firms who specialise in church and mission supplies are moving into the provision of computers, and whilst they may not have the expertise to offer detailed technical assistance, they do give the advantages of dealing with a supplier used to churches, and their service may well be at least as good as from a high street multiple (apart from the local convenience).

Use of professional advice

No church would consider anything beyond a very minor building operation without the services of an architect, and similarly a church looking for a computer system that involves anything other than straightforward applications with common church software and hardware would do well to obtain professional advice in the implementation of a computer system.

By involving an experienced consultant in the selection and implementation of a system, a church can greatly increase the likelihood of choosing the right system for their needs and putting it to work reasonably quickly.

Qualified computer consultants naturally charge fees on an hourly or daily basis similar to other professionals, so the cost is not trivial, but most of those who specialise in working with churches and charitable organisations tend to try to keep below full commercial rates, and are usually prepared to undertake single day assignments (or even less) to keep costs within reason. They are also aware that the cost of any system proposed must be geared to what is realistic for a church.

It is often suggested that for any task it is well worth spending around 10 per cent of the total anticipated cost on professional advice, and this is certainly true with a computer system of any complexity. If the consultant is to provide installation and training services as well, the total cost may be nearer 20 per cent.

However, a good consultant may well be able to save a church considerably more than this by avoiding the costs of choosing a wrong system which fails to achieve what was intended. In some cases, particularly with larger installations, there may be direct savings, as dealers may agree to give discounts if they know a consultant is providing assistance, or they may agree to pay the consultant a commission (which a reputable consultant will pass back to the client in the form of reduced fees).

But just as only a few architects have experience with church buildings, only a few computer professionals have experience of church systems, and it is important not to assume that any computer person in the congregation will be able to assist. The majority of full time computer personnel work on large mainframe applications and have very limited experience of microcomputers. Even if they do have experience of small machines, they are unlikely to have experience of church applications. Computer people in the church may well be of help in assisting the users of the chosen system, and may be able to offer advice about reputable local dealers to supply the hardware. But they will rarely be able to advise on choice of software (except for general purpose applications such as word processing) or on issues of computing as a matter of church strategy.

It is thus well worth considering the use of a computer consultant, preferably with experience in church applications, but at the very least with experience of personal computers in non-commercial organisations.

The qualifications of consultants are important if their advice is to be dependable, as unlike other professions, there is nothing to stop any firm or individual calling themselves computer consultants, and some who do so are no more than hardware dealers on the one hand, or computer hobbyists on the other.

The qualification for a chartered practitioner in the computer field (equivalent to a chartered accountant or chartered architect, for example) is membership of the British Computer Society (MBCS or FBCS). Alternatively, membership of the Institute of Data Processing Management (MIDPM) indicates significant expertise, even though not chartered. Independently owned firms with experience as computer consultants may well belong to the Association of Independent Computer Specialists (AICS) or the Association of Professional Computer Consultants (APCC). Failing any of these, a relevant university degree may be considered. But in addition to qualifications, any consultant must have experience in the size of system considered, and in work with churches or similar organisations.

Most of the specialist church software suppliers offer a consultancy service, and although they cannot be considered 100 per cent independent, particularly with regard to their software, they are required to declare any interests, if they belong to the relevant organisations mentioned above. If a church thinks a firm's software may be applicable, no one will know it better than the firm who developed it, and they will be better able to advise on how it should be used and on the choice of appropriate hardware, than anyone else. Furthermore, if a consultancy firm realises their own software would be inappropriate, they are hardly going to risk their reputation by pressing it in an unsuitable situation. By contrast, they may be able to agree to modify their software to meet a specific need, at considerably less cost than asking an outside firm to develop something from scratch.

Lists of consultants can be obtained from the professional associations above, or from directories held in libraries, and by careful searching it may be possible to identify those with appropriate expertise.

As a general rule, the involvement of a consultant (even if only for a single day) would be very desirable if any of the following apply:

- more than one computer likely to be needed (a consultant must be considered *essential* if there are plans to interconnect them in any kind of network)

- major applications outside those considered in chapter 2, or known unusual requirements for any application

- uncertainty about the right applications to computerise

- applications that can only be implemented with databases or other software requiring extensive installation to meet a particular use

- complex requirements for printed output

- where advice is needed about how the system will fit into church life

- a church larger than those for which the established church software packages are designed

- where the system must be chosen and implemented by persons with no prior understanding at all (for example by someone who has not even read this book!)

- where there are likely to be more than about three different people who will use the system

- where extensive training is likely to be wanted
- if a hard disk system appears to be needed and the users have no previous computer experience (the consultant will advise on configuration and backup procedures)
- where there is a need for automatic transfer of information from one application to another
- in a situation where a number of churches wish to choose a common approach for standardisation (this is much to be recommended)
- if the new system must interconnect to an existing computer application (internal or external), or where data must be transferred automatically from an existing system to a new one.

Points for discussion

1. What are the relative advantages of general purpose and church specific software?

2. What are the likely consequences of choosing hardware without prior consideration of software?

3. To what extent do we want a printer attached to a church computer to give the impression that no computer is being used?

4. In what ways does your church use outside professionals? Would you wish to add computer consultancy to the other fields in which professional advice is sought?

4
Finding the cost and gaining agreement _____

The possible benefits of computers in church life are now widely accepted. A significant number of churches are already using serious computer systems in their work, and a great many more would like to do so.

However, getting from this appreciation to actually acquiring a system and putting it to use can be an uphill struggle in some churches. This is usually due to two issues, often closely related: how to find the purchase costs, and how to convince the church council or equivalent body that a computer system is the right way forward.

Acquiring a system

In some cases, computer systems will be purchased by individual ministers for use in their own ministry, and the involvement of church councils may not be needed. This possibility is discussed further at the end of the chapter. However, when an actual church system is considered, for use across many aspects of church life, it is rarely possible to proceed without approval of the relevant decision making body.

Moreover, if the computer is to be a major tool at the heart of church life, it would be quite wrong to introduce a change of this kind without the church council's approval, even if no church funds are required.

Persuading a church council to invest in a computer is not merely a financial argument. In some churches, the money may present little obstacle. But even where funds are very tight, there will be other issues that need to be explored, if a church is to make the commitment to a computer system which is necessary for its effective use.

Some churches are fortunate enough or visionary enough that purchases of resources such as computer systems are made reasonably frequently, and in such cases the task of finding the money and gaining approval is not a problem. But this is the exception rather than the rule, and it would be wrong to assume that only these churches are able to benefit from computers.

The majority of this chapter is thus devoted to the strategy for finding the costs and persuading the church council, once an individual believes that a computer system may be the right way forward. Undoubtedly this demands considerable faith, but it also demands practical considerations, and these are outlined in what follows.

Approaching church councils

It is one thing for a lively minister or an active lay person to see the value of a computer in church life, but it is quite another to persuade a church council, whose members may be of widely differing ages and backgrounds, that a computer is right for a church, particularly where there may be many other significant demands on church resources.

As a result of this many ministers and lay people stop short of ever putting a proposal to a church council for the acquisition of a computer system. It seems that for every church that has gone ahead and acquired a system, there are five where the church council *has never even been asked*. For a variety of reasons we are reluctant to ask our church councils to consider serious tools for mission, even when we ourselves are convinced of their value. As a result, our churches are deprived of important systems that could enhance church life and widen their ministry.

A suitably chosen computer system with appropriate church related software, and hardware of a kind that will meet the real demands of church life, can bring an immense difference in church life, in freeing ministers for their essential work, and in widening the opportunities of ministry, mission, and growth.

So if a church council is to be approached for a computer, the first and most fundamental issue is to consider the role of a computer as a major tool, on which the church will come to depend heavily, related to many aspects of its life and work.

This needs a good deal of advance reflection. The discussion questions provided in this book may well be relevant. Unless you can identify some clear benefits that you believe a computer can have for your church or for your ministry, you have no right to ask a church council to consider it. But if such benefits are present, it would be wrong to keep the church council in ignorance of the value that a computer could have.

System proposals

Before the church council can be asked for a computer system, one must establish exactly what system is required. Experience suggests that those who put a specific proposal to their churches, for a *definite system* at a *particular cost*, to be obtained from *named suppliers*, get a much more positive response than those who merely raise the general idea, hoping for some degree of consent.

This requires a good deal of advance work, using the criteria defined in chapter 3. You need to have established the general kind of products required, and you need to have approached one or more suppliers for specific quotations.

If the church's needs appear to be complex, it could be wise to involve a consultant to recommend a system. Although this will involve some initial expense it may be within limits that do not require discussion by the full church council. But even if the full council does have to approve the use of a consultant, a definite proposal to involve a particular consultant is likely to receive a positive response, particularly if it is made clear that the consultant may well not recommend a computer at all. Subsequently, if the consultant professionally recommends that a computer system would be of benefit, that will provide a very strong case when the church council considers the system proposed.

There is, of course, no point in involving a consultant purely for persuasive purposes – one must be prepared to accept the consultant's advice. In one case, the author was asked to assist in recommending a system, but his conclusion, in view of the church organisation and attitudes of others involved, was that the church would be unlikely to derive any benefit from a computer at that time.

Costing the system

It is important that any system proposed will actually do the job.

Nothing could be more destructive than getting approval for a given system, only to have to return to the church council a year later to ask for a new system because the original one proved inadequate (which has happened to a number of churches). Far better to go back a year later and say that the original system has proved so valuable, that it is desired to buy some additional software (for example) to extend the computer's areas of use!

In choosing a computer system one naturally wants to be economical and avoid wasting the church's money. But proposing a system that will not really do the job, or where the support from the supplier is likely to be inadequate, could be the biggest waste of all. So consider the alternatives carefully. In practice most churches will not require any more convincing to buy one system that costs 25 per cent more than another, so if you feel the more sophisticated system would actually meet needs better, it is probably the better recommendation. One will be able to defend it better, when questions are asked.

Having said that, there is also much to be said for having two fairly similar alternative proposals, and allowing the church council to decide between them (for example, two systems based on essentially the same software and hardware but with different models of printer). Choose them so that it is clear the larger system would be preferable, but the smaller one would be adequate, and state this to the council. A choice is good because it proves that you are allowing the church some role in the system selection, without expecting them to enter areas outside their competence. Experience suggests that when this is done, the majority of church councils opt for the more expensive system.

One cannot, however, expect a church council to decide between two systems at radically different prices, such as where one costs twice or three times as much as the other. If you say the lower priced system would be adequate, they will doubt your sense in raising the larger proposal at all. If you say the cheaper one is not really adequate, they will again doubt your sense in proposing it. The church council cannot have the expertise to assess the benefits to the church of such inconsistent proposals, and are likely to reject the idea of a computer at all.

In costing your proposed systems, be sure to include *everything* that would have to be covered in the initial costs. This may well include:

- computer
- monitor
- keyboard

- printer
- accessories for printer: cable, tractor feed, etc
- computer operating system software
- software for general applications
- software for church specific applications
- initial supplies of disks, stationery, etc
- furniture
- additional power point
- first year's maintenance and insurance
- training
- delivery
- ongoing support
- VAT, if not included in the prices above.

Some of these items are considered in more detail in chapter 5. Not all will be needed in every case, not all will be priced separately, and many churches will simply consider stationery, maintenance, etc as part of ongoing church expenditure. But failure to consider the total cost is likely to lead to a lot of problems. A great many clergy have made the mistake of thinking about computers in hardware cost alone.

Financing the system

It may seem strange to decide about finance *before* asking the church council. But in practice there are many different ways a church might seek to meet the cost of a system, and realistic options must be identified before a church council can be asked to make a decision. Possible approaches include the following.

Ordinary church funds

In many cases, the computer can simply be funded out of ordinary church income, albeit as an extraordinary item. Only in very small churches, or where a very large system is proposed, will the purchase of a computer account for much more than 10 per cent of yearly income. If the benefits are clear, and giving is at a realistic level, the council will in all probability be happy to accept this.

If the church cannot afford to find the cost out of a single year's collections, it may be better to regard the system as being spread over several years. Perhaps one could set up a fund and repay it over three to five years. Few churches would be unable to afford one fifth of the cost per annum.

Alternatively, churches that prepare advance budgets will naturally want to consider the likely need for a computer when the following year's budgets are being prepared. If the principle of a computer system has been agreed in a budget, the actual decision becomes much easier on a financial level.

One also needs to put costs into perspective. A computer system can seem a lot of money if compared to other items for church *administration*. This is the big mistake that many people make in asking their churches to fund a computer system. Although a computer has administrative benefits, its role in church life will go much wider than this. All members of the church should see the benefits of better communication, more exciting outreach, and more systematic pastoral care. The introduction of a computer system is a major development in church life, and as such is more appropriately compared to a building alteration. Yet very little can be done to the building for the cost of a computer. Even if one only compares the computer with other *tools* in church life – such as a minister's car – it is still very attractive financially. Discussing a computer system in this light can make it much easier for a church council to support it realistically.

Church reserves and ancillary income

Even in churches where income is very tight, there may be money held in reserve for special purposes. In some cases, the computer may be just the special purpose required. Churches are rightly reluctant to use reserves for day to day needs, but a major new development such as the use of a computer, which could lead to growth in church life, may be entirely appropriate.

Alternatively, if a church is unable to fund a computer out of ordinary congregational gifts – perhaps on the grounds that it goes beyond the usual application of church collections – there can be little objection to funding the system from *other* income, such as church fees for weddings, interest on money invested, or rents from letting of premises. A computer is, after all, very valuable for following up marriage contacts, for organising finance, and for managing correspondence about lettings, and it may seem more appropriate to charge it to these areas.

Legacies are another possibility. When a church receives a legacy, the wish is often expressed from the deceased person that the gift be used in some way to further the work of the church. What better way than to buy a computer system?

Individual giving

Quite a number of churches have acquired a computer system as the result of a very generous gift from one person, which has covered a large part of the cost. Even if it covers only part of the total figure, a church council would find it difficult to refuse to provide the balance if it was known that a single gift of (say) half the total cost had already been offered.

Covenants are another possibility. The tax gains to the church through deeds of covenants are well known, but there may be all kinds of difficulties in practice once a church begins to seek large numbers of covenants. This is one way the computer can help find its own cost; with software for managing deeds of covenant it becomes very little extra work to handle a hundred covenants instead of ten.

If a church council cannot find the cost of a system out of ordinary funds, there can be little objection to setting up a special fund and seeking donations from the congregation. Experience suggests that in such cases, a relatively small number of people may be called to make quite generous donations, and the cost may be found.

Many churches find a specific gift day to be of value, but they are not always successful if the money is just placed in ordinary church funds. If the income from a gift day is specifically designated for a computer system, with a definite target to raise, and plenty of information about how it will be used in church life, this can be a relatively straightforward means of finding the money. One can even identify all the different components of the system – right down to individual spare diskettes – and invite various people or groups to buy specific items.

Include the computer with other appropriate costs

The computer is not an object that will run the church in its own right, but will be used by *people*: clergy, secretaries, etc. Where such people are church staff, it is much more natural to include the equipment they use as part of staff costs, rather than treat it entirely separately.

After all, a computer is a relatively small item compared to a year's salary even for one person. In industry it is normal to include substantial overheads with personnel costs, to cover office space, furniture, equipment, services, and there has been an increasing tendency to consider clergy costs as a single figure inclusive of accommodation and travelling expenses. Failure to account this way has led to many church employees being drastically deprived of equipment needed to do their job. Viewed as a small percentage increase in staff costs, a computer may be financed much more easily than if seen as a separate item.

In other cases, churches say they cannot consider a computer because of another project such as a building scheme. Yet very often that scheme includes facilities such as a church office, with no provision for equipment that the office will require. In such cases it is wholly right to include the computer system within the overall project. And in practical terms, it may be much less difficult to add a small amount to a large project than to find that amount on its own.

Consider possible savings

No one is happy about the current shortage of ministers in many churches, and it is always a great loss when a church or group of churches loses a minister. But where salaries are paid locally, such loss may release money previously used for a minister's salary, and this could be used to purchase computer systems to support the remaining clergy. Whilst a computer can in no way make up for losing a minister, it can assist the remaining ministers to be as efficient as possible, and make better use of their time.

From time to time it is necessary to sell church property, as for example when two churches merge, or when a parsonage is no longer required. This is far easier to accept if it is known that the proceeds of the sale will be used in a way that will really benefit the church – as when a church office is set up, incorporating a computer system.

The church computer system may also serve to render other items redundant. Your home computer can perhaps be disposed of. The old manual typewriter may not be needed if it is planned to do all future correspondence with word processing. The duplicator may perhaps be felt unnecessary if the church plans to photocopy or litho print from the computer output. If the church has an addressing machine it can be retired. Look for items such as these that can be sold to help finance the system.

Furthermore, although the main reason for a church to acquire a computer is usually for the new opportunities opened up, there may be some direct savings to be made on existing costs as a result of computerisation.

For example, some churches pay to have their magazine prepared by an outside firm. If so, the word processing facility of the computer may make this unnecessary. Is the church employing anyone to undertake administrative work that will become much quicker by computer? If so, one would not recommend making the person redundant, but the time for which he or she is now released for other work should be put into your calculations as a saving. Is the church paying an agency (denominational or otherwise) some commission to administer deeds of covenant? Possibly this could be saved with an internal system, and give the church greater control.

Sometimes money is separated into different bank accounts simply for administrative convenience; i.e. the only money in the deposit account is set aside for a particular purpose. With appropriate software to assist the church treasurer, this problem may be removed; the computer will keep track of how much money is kept for each purpose, and as much money as is free can then be placed on deposit. In some cases, this can lead to quite significant increases in interest received, that can help pay for the system.

Support from outside bodies

Some charities or trusts may be prepared to make donations to a church to cover the cost of a computer system – or at least contribute towards it. Few national organisations are able to help, but smaller local organisations – even trusts within the auspices of the church, perhaps set up from historic legacies – may be able to support the purchase of a church computer system. Church computing could be relevant, for example, to trusts with purposes of evangelism, support of pastoral work, or education.

Local firms, too, may not be keen on giving donations to repair the church roof, but may be much more enthusiastic about making gifts that will enable the church to use modern technology.

In certain cases there may be quite legitimate tax advantages to a firm to buy a computer system and give it to the church, rather than give a donation. Some firms have trusts specifically to offer this kind of help. But one must insist on choosing the system the church needs. Be very wary of accepting gifts of equipment that industry is throwing out; such machines are most unlikely to be able to run the software required.

Running costs

Any proposal must also be clear about running costs if the council is interested in these. Much will depend on the kind of maintenance arrangements felt necessary. This is discussed further in chapter 8.

System usage and timescale

In putting a proposal to the church council, various practical issues must also have been resolved. The key questions here are: where will the system be located, and who will use it? These points are considered further in chapters 5, 6, and 9, but there are some early considerations in approaching a church council.

Selection of users

In smaller churches, the minister will often be the main user, with the computer being in the parsonage study, but it is still right and proper that the system should be owned by the church, wherever possible. If the minister has a secretarial assistant, he or she may also use it to some extent. But there is no point in this case in claiming that the system will be of benefit to the church treasurer, for example, unless the minister is genuinely able to make the system available for that purpose.

Slightly larger churches are increasingly setting up offices on church premises, and in such cases the church office is the natural location. If the church has, or plans to have, a full time church secretary or administrator they would then be the main user. But if several people work in the office on different occasions, one needs to be quite clear about who would use the system, and for what purposes. A proposal that the computer be available to anyone, is likely to be considered too vague and unworkable by the church council.

This implies that you will have discussed the proposal for a computer with those who will be the main users, well before the matter is considered at a church council. You will probably have taken them to see any demonstrations of the proposed software, or at the very least, you will have let them peruse the supplier's literature in detail. Some people are always a little anxious about using something new until they actually get down to it, but you must overcome any serious doubts they have before you can honestly recommend a system to the council.

The church also needs to have one person who will have overall responsibility for the system – to act as a computer co-ordinator. Failure to identify someone in this role can lead to problems once the system is in use, and can rightly lead to concern from the church council at the stage when the system is considered.

If one or more of the intended users of the system is a member of the church council, their support is vital. They will be able to back up any proposal as regards the likely benefits of the system, and will help overcome any concerns that the system might not be used properly or effectively. If they are not on the council, they could perhaps be asked to attend for a specific meeting, to answer possible questions. But if likely users are members of the council and have received little or no advance consultation, they are likely to discourage the council from proceeding.

Timing

The timescale for implementation of any proposed system must also be determined before a proposal is put to the church council. Lack of a clear timescale is likely to lead to indefinite postponement of a decision, or endless referral to committees and working parties. A few churches that believe in long range planning have successfully budgeted for computers some while ahead, but in most churches, the decision can only be made effectively if the system is to be purchased more or less immediately after approval is given.

To plan a timescale needs considerable care. It definitely helps to focus the mind if there is something specific coming up for which the computer will make a great deal of difference. It is very useful to be able to say: "We really must have the system up and working by April to process the deed of covenant claims for this year" or "If we aren't properly set up by September, we won't be able to make use of the system for sorting out the autumn housegroups".

The majority of the work will be done *before* the proposal ever reaches the church council, in researching possible systems and prices. Once one has a definite proposal, a decision is needed as quickly as possible, because products are changing all the time, as explained in chapter 3, and a delay of a few months might mean starting research again from scratch. But the church also needs to allow a while after the system is received for initial familiarisation and entry of data. Detailed advice on preparation of an implementation plan is given in chapter 6.

Committees

It is, of course, important to take the proposal to the correct meeting. Some churches have a complex committee structure to navigate. In larger churches, it may be that the real proposal is put to (say) the finance committee, who will exercise the detailed decisions, and simply agree a system for formal approval by the church council. Other denominations will hold the main discussion in a deacons' meeting and seek final approval at a church meeting. Whatever the correct path, it is important to ensure that the main discussion only takes place once, if at all possible, otherwise one has to repeat the same ground and possibly aggravate those with minor concerns into raising major obstacles. If it is known that the initial meeting would only hold a preliminary discusion and the main decision would be made at the full council, it would be better to raise the matter 'for information only' in the first instance.

If the matter will need consideration in committees, this must be allowed for in the timescale. But at all costs avoid endless referrals between different meetings. Avoid, too, setting up special working parties unless they will be genuinely helpful in getting the final approval. If a working party is essential, give it a maximum of a month to complete its work, otherwise its initial meetings will be meaningless. But working parties created simply to allow all those interested to have a say do not usually help the objective very much!

Putting the issue to the council

Up and down the country there are literally hundreds of ministers and leading laity looking into the possibility of a computer for their church. Most find that they very quickly appreciate the benefits that a computer system could bring. But despite this confidence, many are very reluctant to put a definite proposal to the church council to go ahead and purchase a system.

This is surprising because the author is not aware in five years experience of church computing of a single case where a *definite costed proposal* for a church computer has been rejected by a church council. There are one or two cases where a working party decided not to make any immediate proposal to the council, or where a church council failed to approve a system that had already been bought by an individual. But there are a great many more cases where no proposal has so far been put.

What are the reasons then why ministers and others are reluctant to propose to their church council that a computer system be purchased? There seem to be three main ones.

Lack of money is the most common uncertainty. People feel their church council would not be prepared even to consider finding the money for a system, so they do not even ask.

A second problem is the luxury view, particularly where the main user will be the minister. People fear that the church council will see it as wanting the church to pay out for the minister to have a personal toy.

The third area of doubt is more subtle, and is based on a general concern about personal data and technology. The proposal is not put because of concern that the church council will object to whole idea of a computer as being the wrong approach to handling personal information, or because of worries about general anti-technology fears among council members.

Getting the council's approval

If computers are to be used effectively in churches as real tools we must overcome these doubts and find ways to ask church councils to approve computer systems where they are clearly appropriate.

One cannot pretend to a church council that a computer is a minor item. If a computer is to be a serious tool involved in the life, communication and mission of a church then the church council must be enabled to consider it at that level. It may well need a church council meeting devoted almost entirely to the computer issue – certainly without any other expenditure matters on the agenda.

A clearly produced written report is also needed, circulated in advance of the meeting to all members, explaining the system proposed, method of financing, main users, system location, and timescale. There is then no doubt about what is sought. If one tried to present all this orally, one would be speaking for half an hour and most of the points would be forgotten. The meeting itself should simply be used to explain the benefits in church life. A well produced proposal is evidence that the idea has been well thought out – even if not everyone reads it – and it shows that a computer is not a minor issue.

If the council is approached with a definite costed proposal, for a specific configuration of software and hardware at a specific overall price, one is asking for a concrete decision. It is not the task of a church council to make technical decisions between widely differing alternative systems. The task of a church council is to decide whether to take certain steps forward in the life of the church.

This requires that the proposal is viable and really will do what is claimed. If software has been chosen that is designed for church work, reliable hardware selected with adequate capacity, and it is proposed to deal with reputable suppliers, it will be much easier to tell the church council that this is the system the church needs. If one tries to propose a rather limited setup on a trial basis that will probably need enhancing in six months what confidence can they have to make a strategic decision in church life?

On the personal and technological issues, a lot depends on careful explanation of exactly how the computer will be used. It is important to choose software that will have good control of confidentiality and to make clear that members will be allowed to see their own entry (though not other people's). Describe what the precise benefits will be: better newsletters, more systematic pastoral visiting, easier membership lists for organisations, better use of church finance, freeing of ministers and leading lay people for what they should be doing. Always aim for openness and understanding. (It is to allow the exploration of these kind of points that a full church council meeting is needed to consider the issues.)

Finally, encourage the church council to consider the whole issue prayerfully – as it should with any issue. But there can sometimes be a tendency to feel that technology and prayer have little to do with each other and that such decisions can be taken purely on practical considerations.

Nothing could be further from the truth. Experience indicates that when a church council is asked positively to consider a computer on a careful and prayerful basis, with the issues clearly explained, then if a decision is taken to proceed the money is often found very willingly, and any general objections fall easily into place. Sometimes it is even the church council that is leading the way in wanting to support the minister with the resources for effective ministry.

Ultimately, though, one must be prepared to accept the council's decision. The biggest fear we have when we look to our church councils is the fear of rejection. We feel they may reject our proposal for a computer, and so we fail to raise it. There is no doubt that there is a personal disappointment when we work hard on something only to find it rejected by a meeting, but we need to stop ourselves feeling *personally* rejected in such cases.

If one has done all the preparation listed above and the council still says "no", then, if we believe in the right of our church councils to make decisions, we must be prepared to accept that. If we only raise proposals that we believe are bound to succeed, we are denying the council its right to exercise judgement in church life.

Objections

There are, nevertheless, a number of questions or objections that may be raised in response to one's proposal, before the church council takes a decision. Responding positively to these is vital if the council is to be able to take a positive decision.

A few objections may be raised by members wishing to be awkward, and in such cases it is probably better to amplify the benefits rather than respond directly. (For ministers, this may be easier if they are not chairing meetings themselves.) But most objections will represent a genuine query or concern and if you can sympathise with the point but show that it is not a problem, you are likely to gain support.

A number of objections have already been discussed, but the following is a list of some of the more common points that arise, and some brief suggestions of ways of responding.

"We can't afford it!"   If you have planned how the system is to be financed, you will have a precise response. If an appeal is to be launched, no one will know the result until it takes place. If the cost is to be met from ordinary church funds, you will have established either that the money is available, or that it could be found with only marginal increases in giving.

"Why spend all that when you can get an XXX machine in the high street for only £YYY?"   This objection usually comes from computer hobbyists. You need to explain carefully that a church system is not a hobby system, that it needs proper software for the job, a supplier who will offer full support, hardware that will stand up to church use, and it needs to be suitable for use by people without computer expertise. (You will also usually find that they are not really comparing like with like, and that their system would cost at least £YYY plus 50 per cent if they were to include all items on your list. But it is not usually worth getting into discussions of this kind as they miss the point and are boring to others present.) You will usually find that others with a vision of church strategy will support you in the need for a proper system.

"I know a very good machine or supplier that I use in my work, and I would like to recommend that."   It is always helpful to know of people who have experience with personal computers, and if they are sympathetic their help may be valuable when you are getting to know your system – acknowledging this contribution is probably useful. But if the research has been done thoroughly and you are confident of the system and supplier proposed, you will normally know why you are proposing your system. Very probably the system they use is suitable for their work, but probably would not support the software you need. Point out the value of software designed for church work and of using a supplier who understands church needs.

"I am employed as a computer programmer. Could I have a chance to study the proposal and make some comments at a later date?"   This objection comes in various forms from computer professionals who feel excluded. Yet it is very hard to include everyone, and the number of a computer people around is such that most churches will have at least someone in the field. The problem is to identify those whose expertise is relevant, as explained in chapter 3. Moreover, different computer people have different opinions about products, and you could go on for ever. Certainly they are unlikely to have experience of church applications, whereas you will have studied these carefully. So it is unlikely that their choice of system would be better than yours, and the church council as a whole needs to see that their

request would delay the whole process. The very worst misunder-standings are from computer people who feel they would like to write programs for you themselves, which could lead to enormous delays, lack of support, lack of documentation, etc. At all costs encourage the rest of the council to see that 'DIY computing' is not the way forward for strategic church use.

"What about the Data Protection Act?" Essentially there is no problem in keeping personal information on computer provided the church complies with the Act, which is not difficult if a suitable system is chosen and the church registers what is being done with it. In fact the Act is a definite advantage because it removes any concerns about personal data being used for improper purposes. This issue is considered in detail in chapter 7.

"Doesn't it need too much technical knowledge for our people to be able to use it?" If a good system has been chosen with user friendly software and where the supplier will provide some initial training and ongoing support, there should be little difficulty in answering this. Ideally, the potential users will actually have seen a demonstra-tion and had a go, so you will know if they can cope. Point out that a good computer system does not need technical knowledge to use it.

"I can see that a word processor might be useful, but a computer seems a bit too much for where we are at." Explain that the computer will include word processing, but that it can handle many other applications as well. A serious stand-alone word processor could cost a good deal more and would not have all the other facilities that a computer could give.

"What are we doing thinking of computers and such like? What we need for our church is more: preaching/visiting/young people/building work/ return to traditional standards . . ." This point is usually raised by someone who has not understood the benefits of a computer in church life and who feels threatened by the idea of a computer as something they cannot comprehend. A reference to the benefits that computers have had in other churches may help, either in local experience or from publications (see appendix). Point out that they will not personally have to use the system. You cannot usually get such people to the point of appreciating the benefits until they see the system in use, even though a system will probably have some impact on all the areas they believe to be of higher priority! It is best simply to ask them to take it on trust that you have investigated the possibilities thoroughly and are convinced that the system would be of value.

"I can see that computers may be all right for big churches but surely not for situations like ours!" Point out that a computer can bring significant benefits to any church. In practice it seems that any situation where a minister has care of more than a hundred members may benefit, even if the members are spread over several churches. If possible, cite other churches of similar size that are using a computer system effectively, even if they are not personally known to you. Indicate that you are convinced of the benefits you have stated. (This objection shows that the person can see the value in general terms, but seeks reassurance. Once reassured, the person is likely to support the proposal actively.)

"This is all very well, but couldn't the money be better spent on supporting the third world, for example!" This objection is often raised in response to any items of church expenditure, and rightly so, because the responsibility of the church is to look beyond itself. The ideal answer is always to buy the computer *and* give money away. Making this decision is part of the prayerful process that the church council must undertake. But consistency is also important. There is no point in employing a minister but failing to provide the resources for effective ministry. There is no value in producing a newsletter if the current means of production give an ineffective result. In order for the Church to reach out to the third world and elsewhere, we need local churches to be equipped effectively for ministry and service.

"If we wait till next year it would be cheaper." This point was discussed in detail in chapter 3. By waiting until next year the church would possibly get a *more powerful* system for the same price, but if it is felt that the proposed system would be quite adequate, there is no real benefit in delaying. In general, the longer the church waits, the longer it will be without the benefits that a computer can bring.

"The computer will change how things are organised. I think the present ways are best!" This would indicate that the objector is not persuaded that the new opportunities a computer could bring would actually be beneficial. It may be that the person has spotted a genuine problem in the proposal, which needs further examination. But more likely, it is a general reaction against change or moving forwards. Such a person can best be reassured by pointing out aspects that will *not* change, and by drawing attention to the potential of the system for saving time and releasing people for other work.

Systems purchased by individuals

Whilst it is normally desirable for the church council to be responsible for any system, computers owned by individuals can still be of value in the church. Ministers with their own computers and the right software often find substantial savings in time, or make more systematic use of the time they have, and there may be important new opportunities in their ministry.

Church computers or ministers' computers

There are many advantages in any computer system being owned by the church, and under church control, rather than belonging to the minister or any other individual. The computer cannot be a vehicle of church strategy if it is not managed by the church council. As emphasised in chapter 1, the main argument for the computer is in the management of church information. The church council cannot call for certain reports, or request that certain information be placed on computer, if it is dependent on the willingness of a particular person making equipment available.

There are also many disadvantages in individually owned systems if the individual concerned leaves the church. Any benefits that the church may have gained from the system are lost when the minister or lay owner moves on, and as a result, the machine cannot be used for anything that the church *really depends upon*, unless it is done in such a way that it could easily be transferred back to a manual approach at a later date, which fails to make effective use of the computer as a tool for new possibilities.

Similarly, the applications are usually restricted by the activities of the person concerned. It is not usually possible for the minister's own computer to be used in church finance, for example.

Therefore, whenever there is the slightest chance of getting agreement from the church, there is much to be said for approaching them for the purchase of what would actually be a church computer system.

However, it is accepted that there are many situations where no amount of putting the case carefully and examining sources of funds would enable a church council to agree to acquire a computer. In such cases, if an individual minister is able to purchase a system, for use primarily in his or her own ministry, there is still a great deal to be gained.

This is particularly so when an individual minister is working with several different churches, and where there is no specific relationship between those churches beyond the fact of having a common minister. In such cases, it is rarely viable to have a system jointly owned by four or five different churches, attempting to exercise joint control over how it is used, although it is sometimes possible for the largest church to be the owner, and the other churches contribute to the cost or use it as appropriate. But if this is not the case, a computer system used as a tool for individual ministry, can still offer many of the benefits described in this book.

Financing a minister's computer

For an individual minister to purchase a reliable computer system is often a major commitment, and there is sometimes a temptation to opt for a cheap system without the right software in an effort to economise.

Whilst it is true that an individual minister will probably be able to accept a cheaper screen and printer, for example, than a busy church office, the fundamental requirement to *choose the software, then the hardware* applies to any situation. Systems without the correct software and hardware are very unlikely to save any time for ministers.

Costs have fallen, and a minister's computer, complete with printer and software, now costs much less than a minister's car. But finding the money is still a major concern.

Some ministers buying computer systems will be able to draw on savings. In other cases the money will come from income, and in such cases hire purchase or personal bank loans may enable the cost to be spread over a period, particularly on hardware. Credit agreements are rarely available on software, but some suppliers may be willing to make informal agreements to spread the cost over several months. Buying a basic version of a package and upgrading later may also be a solution.

Even where a church cannot afford the full costs, it is important that the church council is conscious of making some contribution. In such cases, it is often appropriate to ask the church to pay for the software (which will normally be the church-specific element) even if the hardware is being funded by the minister as an individual.

Many ministers have limited personal income from some activity other than their main ministerial work, such as wedding/funeral fees, chaplaincy work, teaching, writing, etc. For many clergy, this has been the source that has made a computer system possible.

Churches unwilling to buy a computer outright may recognise the need to pay realistic monthly expenses to cover their minister's administrative costs. It may be possible to get agreement for a regular amount to be provided in expenses, towards computing costs, in much the same way as ministers' car travel is supported.

A minister who holds some church office at a level beyond the local church (e.g. diocesan youth secretary) may be able to persuade the diocese, district, etc to cover the cost of the system, or at least a part of it. Most ministers who hold offices of this kind have to co-ordinate mailing lists and prepare documents and reports; this will frequently require the same kind of hardware and software as for local church purposes. Certainly the benefit of a computer system to ministers with such responsibilities is very significant indeed.

Tax relief may also be available. Under a certain agreement* (partly to do with a well publicised case involving the former financial controller of IBM, and more specifically due to intensive work by the Church Computer Users Group and the Churches Main Committee) the Inland Revenue has accepted that ministers of religion may be entitled to tax relief on the provision of 'modern technological equipment' (e.g. computers and photocopiers). The allowance would be on the same principle as for other items of a capital nature.

The ruling requires that the equipment is used for normal ministerial duties (e.g. keeping parish records or production of parish magazines) that the minister would otherwise have to carry out by hand. It is generally agreed that serious systems clearly designed for church use will carry more weight than 'home computers' that may not be capable of carrying out serious office tasks. In particular, opinion suggests that systems with hardware and software bought at the same time, where the software is clearly appropriate to ministerial tasks, will gain approval more easily.

The authorities reserve the usual right of considering each case individually, and may ask supplementary questions about the use of the system before any allowance is agreed. However, if approved, a tax allowance will significantly reduce the effective cost of a system for most ministers.

Other individual owners

There may also be cases where a computer will be purchased by an individual other than the minister. A church treasurer, for example, may be prepared to buy a computer system specifically to assist work in church finance. This will be particularly so if the person concerned acts as treasurer of several churches or organisations.

There are also many cases where church members have machines primarily for their secular work, which they are willing to use for church purposes.

*The taxation of ministers of religion: office equipment Churches Main Committee Circular No. 1984/21.

However, church councils need to exercise considerable vigilance over such individually owned systems. Particularly where the church application is secondary to the main reason for buying the hardware, there may be inadequate consideration for software, and the church can be left in a difficult position when that individual retires from office, or if the information is subsequently to be transferred to a church machine.

Whilst there is no reason why an individual should not use his or her own computer to word process a report to the church, or to produce an occasional spreadsheet of church budgets, it is quite another matter when large amounts of church information become held on a computer that is not under church control. If personal information is involved – and this is often the case when records include membership, deeds of covenant, or even details of individual receipts and payments – there are implications under the Data Protection Act (see chapter 7) and ethical concerns about the management of this information.

So, whilst an individual may well be able to serve the church more effectively by using a computer, considerable care is needed, and the implementation of a church owned computer system is certainly to be favoured wherever possible.

Points for discussion

1. What do you feel are the relative advantages of computer systems being owned by the church or by the minister?

2. Many church councils are ill equipped to take major decisions of church strategy. If so, does this mean we should attempt to present a computer as a minor item, and avoid detailed discussion?

3. What would be the most appropriate way to finance a computer system in your own church? What would be a realistic timescale?

4. Are we guilty of declining to raise issues with church councils unless we are almost certain that the council will agree with us?

5
Locating the system ─────────────

The proper site for a church computer system is fundamental to its effective use in church life. One is continually reminded that the church consists of people, not buildings, and this fact is vital in deciding where to locate any system.

Possible locations

The main consideration is who will use it. However, the reverse is also true: the choice of location will, in practice, determine who will be the users. It is through the users of the system that the impact will be felt in the church, so the location is not a minor consideration; it greatly affects the management of information in the church.

The two most common locations are the church office and the minister's study, so we examine these first.

The church office

More and more churches are wishing to free the minister from undue administrative work, and are seeking to provide a focus for co-ordination of church activities, in the form of a church office.

The office may range from a church vestry which is staffed by volunteers for a few hours per week, to a full time centre with extensive equipment and several members of administrative staff.

This is largely influenced by the resources of the particular church, and by the necessity or otherwise for appointment of a church administrator.

If a church office already exists with full time staff, and if it functions as the nerve centre of the local church, it would be absurd to consider any other location for a church computer system. Clearly those who work in the church office would need immediate access to information held on computer and will take responsibility for entry and amendment of information. They will also be responsible for printing listings and other details needed by leaders of the various groups within church life.

In certain cases there may be arguments for additional machines elsewhere (see below), but to site the main system anywhere other than in the church office would seriously handicap the work of the church administrator and others, and the computer would never achieve a strategic role in church life; it might even produce great problems.

The church office as a location has a great deal to commend it, and even if those who work in the office are initially apprehensive about computers, it would be a grave mistake to give the machine instead to an experienced computer user elsewhere. Rather, the church office staff should be offered appropriate training to use the system effectively.

The motives for establishing church offices and for investing in church computer systems are very similar, and often the two go hand in hand. One of the main reasons for establishing a church office is to centralise the management of information, with use of a computer being an important tool in that task.

A church with a full time office and no effective computer system is unlikely to be making the best use of the church administrator's time. Provision of good computer facilities should be regarded as an important requirement when church offices are being established.

Certain applications are almost impossible unless the computer is located on church premises. The most obvious is the recording of regular giving through envelopes; the computer must be sited where the envelopes are counted, or most of the benefits of this application are lost. Use of the computer for teaching purposes would have the same requirement, though often different equipment is used for this purpose.

However, if the church office is only staffed part time, and particularly if there are rotas of different people on different days, it may not be the best location. If the main users will be those staffing the office, then clearly that is a good place, but if the staff are more involved in other activities, and if the office is more a point of contact than the centre of church information, another location may be more appropriate. In particular, where rotas of volunteers are involved, it can be very difficult to have sufficiently effective liaison and training to enable the system to be used efficiently.

Consideration must also be given to access for what may be termed *casual users* – those who require the computer for specific purposes, but who are not going to want a computer on their desk. These may include:

- clergy or leaders of specific groups who simply need occasional use of the system for word processing

- a covenant secretary, who may need several hours use at certain times of year, but at other times will only need very limited use

- the treasurer who may need access for a certain time each week to enter transactions

- the minister who may need access for a short period each day or each week to record visits and produce visiting lists.

Very often the church office is still a good location, because it is central and accessible; if the computer is in someone's home it may be convenient for that person, but very inconvenient for others.

However, if casual users wish to use the system during the day, this must be scheduled carefully, and adequate space must be available so that these users do not disrupt the work of those based in the church office.

Thought is equally needed if casual users require access at evenings and weekends. Some church buildings can be very cold, lonely and inhospitable at these times, and this may not give the right environment for careful work using the computer. If there are to be a large number of such casual users, would security problems arise in having so many keys to the church office? These issues must be carefully examined.

Similarly, church treasurers who have been used to keeping their books in their living rooms may be reluctant about having to travel to the church office to use a computer, and this must be considered sensitively. If the computer system is expected to bring substantial time savings, the treasurer may well feel the additional travel is justified. Alternatively, the treasurer may make some changes of practice, such as recording transactions fortnightly rather than weekly, or using the computer at a time when he or she would be on church premises anyway.

So whilst the church office has many advantages as the location for a computer, there are other factors to consider if use of the system is to be successful.

The minister's study

In those churches without a church office, where the church office has only a very limited function, or where the system is being used to support ministry across more than one church, the minister's study is usually the most obvious location.

This is, of course, on the assumption that the minister is the main user, but this will usually be the case in the majority of churches without an administrator.

In most cases the minister's study is within their home, and is used in that context, though where ministers have an office on church premises, this can be the best choice of all, if the minister is prepared to allow access to others when needed.

The minister's study has many advantages as a location. In terms of the focal role of ministers in church life, it means that information is at hand for pastoral work, leadership, and co-ordination.

Names of new contacts can be entered immediately they are known, particularly for weddings, baptisms, etc. Pastoral visits and new pastoral concerns (if held on computer) can be recorded as soon as they are made. Word processing is available as a personal tool whenever required, and if a sermon is being prepared at 11.30 at night, the computer is on hand. Clearly if the minister had to go to a church office to use such facilities, much less use would be made of them.

The main disadvantage is the inaccessibility for other users. Unless the minister is prepared to open his or her study for use by the treasurer, applications in church finance will not usually be possible. Because the minister has the computer, there may also be a tendency to transfer certain functions to the minister which were previously being done by lay people – magazine editing, for example. If this results in improved standards and if the additional time is small, it may be justified, but in general caution is required to ensure that the minister is not overloaded in this way.

On the other hand, in denominations such as the Roman Catholics where a number of priests may live in the same house, and where finance is often under control of the clergy too, the location of the computer within the clergy residence is often ideal from all respects.

Portable systems

Sometimes a portable computer is proposed as the ideal solution to the problem of location. The computer can be kept in the church office or minister's study most of the time, but carried elsewhere when needed.

There are several snags with this argument. In the first place, highly portable computers tend to be more expensive, and are not always so good for long term use because of poorer screen resolution, for example.

In the second place, it is rarely adequate just to move the computer; one almost always needs the printer as well, together with various disks, paper, cables and manuals. It is rarely possible to get the hardware from a car into a particular room, connect the cables, put paper in the printer, and so on, in much less than 15 minutes, and the same time again to dismantle it. Moreover, if one tries to work too fast, there is considerable risk of accidental damage.

So whilst it might be viable, perhaps, to transfer the machine to the treasurer for a few days each year when end of year accounts are drawn up (which would not require a specifically portable machine) it is highly inconvenient to try to do this every week.

It should be noted that hard disk systems are particularly unsuitable for extensive carrying around, as they are very prone to expensive damage and loss of data due to rough handling.

However, if more than one machine is considered, a portable computer with floppy drives and inexpensive printer is often a good supplement to the main machine in the church office.

Multiple computers

In larger churches, serious consideration must be given to having more than one machine, not only with regard to location, but also because once the system begins to be used effectively, there may be problems of sharing the equipment between all those who want to use it: a personal computer can only be used by one person at a time.

Many people assume that the solution is a central computer with connections to separate terminals (VDUs) for different users.

This approach is often appropriate to large firms with mainframe computer systems that have tens or hundreds of terminals, but it would be a very expensive approach for the local church. However, it is impossible to generalise about such issues as equipment is changing rapidly and the information here is only intended as an overview; any church which believes such a multi-user system may be needed must definitely involve a consultant.

The cheapest approach when more than one person needs computer use at the same time (or in different locations) is simply to have two or more computers. It is very much cheaper and simpler to buy two separate computers than to purchase a multi-user computer that can support two users simultaneously.

In such cases, the two machines should be compatible in terms of being able to run the same software from the same type of diskettes. It is thus a simple matter to transfer information from one machine to another, simply by transferring a diskette. This approach can also be used to communicate with those at considerable distance (diocesan offices or denominational headquarters, for example) simply by putting a diskette in the post.

Often the second machine is less expensive than the main one. For example, the church office may have a major system with a hard disk, to keep large membership files, and a high speed, high quality printer. A minister in the church might be provided with a floppy disk machine with a low cost printer to use for personal word processing. When a high quality print is needed for something important, the document diskette is simply brought into the church office and printed there. An additional machine might be provided for church finance, on the same lines.

In such cases, the extra machine can often serve as a useful backup if the main computer is out of order, and it may be possible to economise on maintenance this way, though of course large files held on the hard disk are only accessible once the main machine is repaired.

For such schemes to work, it is necessary to have the same software on each machine; for example, if a document is prepared on one machine using a certain word processing package, that same word processing software must also be available on the computer used when the document is to be printed. Remember, too, that most software licences only cover use on one machine (see chapter 3) and in general a second licence or a second copy of the package must be purchased for the second machine. You are free to copy *your own data* from one machine to another, but copying software in this way is highly illegal.

Great care must be taken, though, to avoid having multiple copies of important files of information. For example, suppose a membership file is held on the church office computer, and the minister takes a copy for his or her own computer to plan some visiting. So far, so good. But then some visit notes are added to the minister's copy of the file. In the meantime, a couple of changes of address have been noted on the church office central list. There are now two files around, with different information, but with equal claims to being up to date.

The problem is one of duplicated data, which is one of the major issues that computer professionals always seek to avoid in designing systems. As soon as data is duplicated, there is always a risk that it will be altered in one place and not in another, and no one will know what is correct. The result can produce havoc for information management in the church, and the situation can be even worse than it was with numerous inconsistent pieces of paper passing around before introduction of the computer.

It is therefore wise for central information such as church lists and details of financial transactions to be held in one place only. As far as possible, resist the temptation to take copies: use the central system, or produce a printed listing to take away. Everyone knows that a printed listing is only up to date on the date when it was produced (good software will show the date of issue on all listings) and whilst people may scribble amendments on the listing, they know that details must in due course be communicated to whoever is responsible for the central system. It is almost always possible to work on this basis, but if it is essential to take a copy of a key file for work on a second machine, it must be strictly on the understanding that it is for inspection only, that no amendments are to be made, and that the copy is to be deleted immediately it is no longer required.

In a large church office it may be appropriate to have two or more computers, normally set aside for different applications, perhaps one for membership work and finance and another for word processing.

For a small proportion of very large church offices, this approach is impossible, as the scale of work is such that several staff genuinely need access to the same files at more or less the same time. In such cases, a multi-user system is essential, but rather than have one computer with separate terminals, it is usually more effective to have a number of separate personal computers connected together in such a way that they can share access to the printer and to a hard disk containing key files. However, it is still possible to run programs on each machine separately. This approach is called a *local area network* (LAN), and professional advice is undoubtedly required, as there are many technical problems. In particular, most church software is not currently designed to work on a multi-user basis with several people attempting to amend information in the same file at the same time.

It would in theory be possible to have a network connecting equipment in several different locations in the parish. Such a network spread across more than one site is called a *wide area network* (WAN), and information is transferred between sites using telephone lines, with a device known as a *modem* being used at each end to convert information to and from a suitable form for transmission by telephone line. For long periods of use, permanent lines must be leased from British Telecom, though if connection is required for less than about an hour a day it may be viable to dial up another computer using the ordinary telephone network.

For some people this is the dream of the ultimate technological church, and there is almost a genre of ecclesiastical science fiction

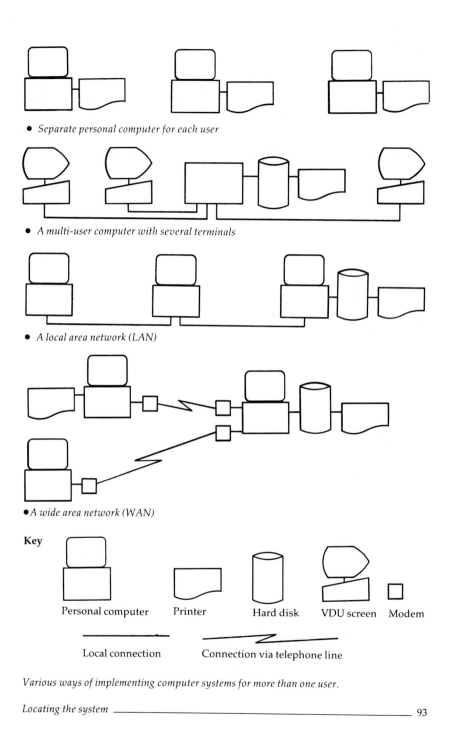

• *Separate personal computer for each user*

• *A multi-user computer with several terminals*

• *A local area network (LAN)*

•*A wide area network (WAN)*

Key

Personal computer   Printer   Hard disk   VDU screen   Modem

Local connection   Connection via telephone line

Various ways of implementing computer systems for more than one user.

based on people staying at home and even taking part in worship through computer communication.

Unfortunately, even at a serious level, there are many practical problems to the use of WANs in churches, the main one being the very heavy costs of telephone lines and calls (quite apart from the extensive hardware costs) which in most cases simply make the whole idea unfeasible. It is hard to see WANs being used in the strategy of the local church in the present century.

There are some applications, though, which may warrant use of modems and telephone lines to communicate information outside the local church. Various electronic mail facilities (including telex) can now be used by means of a personal computer and modem, and there are certain major databases of information which it is possible to access in this way. Similarly, with suitable communications software, modems can be useful for urgent transfer of information between incompatible computers or between systems at considerable distance.

Undoubtedly such applications will increase, but they can be complicated to get working, and can easily become a luxury for those interested in computers for their own sake, rather than in the real service of the church. There are few situations in inter-church communication where the sending of a diskette by first class post would be too slow, and this is immeasurably cheaper and simpler than the use of telecommunications.

The chosen environment

It is well worth giving some thought to establishing the best environment for any computer system, whether it is to be in a fully equipped parish office or in a corner of the minister's study.

Before any equipment is delivered, it is vital to see that all items are properly covered on insurance against fire and theft, and accidental damage if you feel it necessary – though see also chapter 8 regarding maintenance.

The next thought is furniture: a surface is needed on which to place the computer and printer. A table about 4 ft by 2 ft is acceptable, though if you have the space, something at least 6 in wider and deeper will allow more room for papers and manuals while the machine is in use, and will give space to put the keyboard a convenient distance away from the screen.

A table is much better than a desk, as the drawer unit of a desk gets in the way of the printer paper fed from underneath, and can also restrict leg room for the operator. Purpose-designed computer workstations are available which have a slot in the surface for the printer paper, so that the paper feeding up into the printer does not get tangled with the paper coming down. However, the prices sometimes charged for such items can be astronimical, and one needs to evaluate them carefully.

At all costs try to avoid taking up a lot of space with a computer on someone's normal working desk – it will get in the way when not in use.

An adjustable chair is also quite helpful so that users can get the best position. You will also need a convenient shelf or cupboard for diskettes and manuals; if many people have access to the office, these should be locked away when not in use.

Try to avoid placing the equipment in front of a window (a bright window surrounding the screen makes for eye strain) or with a window directly behind the operator, which will give a lot of reflections. It is a good idea to put the computer against a wall at right angles to any windows, especially if it can be in a shady corner. If there are a lot of problems with reflections on the screen, it is well worth investing in window blinds or an anti-reflective screen filter. At all costs, try to avoid direct sunlight on the screen; it is almost impossible to work under these conditions, and it can cause damage to the equipment. With south facing windows nearby, blinds are more or less essential.

Another factor in avoiding eye strain is to use the all-important brightness control on the computer's monitor. If the screen is too dim in the daytime, the user will struggle to see what is displayed. But if it is left at the day level in the evening, when surroundings are much darker, one can quickly get dazzled. This issue is more important in churches, where machines are likely to be used in day and evening, than in other organisations where machines may only be at use in the working day. The brightness control should be pointed out to all who have cause to use the system. Keep the screen clean of dust and fingermarks – kits are available for this purpose.

If you have purchased a good quality monitor and use it at the right brightness, and users experience strain or headaches, they should be advised to visit an optician, as computer screens can occasionally highlight undetected eye problems.

Having chosen a location, nearby power points are needed. Cables trailing across the room are not only dangerous to users, but can easily get pulled out while the system is in use, leading to serious loss of data. For the same reason, multi-way adaptors are definitely best avoided, although a proper multi-way trail socket that is neatly tucked away may well be acceptable. You will probably need at least two sockets – one for the computer and one for the printer. Some

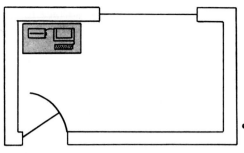

● *Good. No direct light can fall on the screen.*

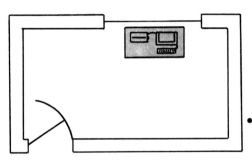

● *Bad. The operator will be badly distracted by the bright window behind the screen.*

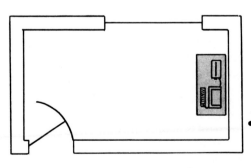

● *Acceptable. There will be some reflections on the screen but only at a wide angle.*

Good and bad positions for a computer in relation to the window in a room.

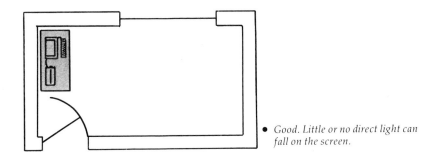

● *Good. Little or no direct light can fall on the screen.*

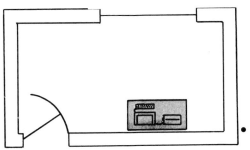

● *Bad. There will be severe reflections on the screen from the window.*

machines need a third socket for the monitor. Check with the hardware supplier and plan accordingly. Once the system is installed, be sure that cables do not get in the way of the printer paper, or you may get printer jams. It can be helpful to tape cables out of the way to the underside of the table.

Static electricity can harm computer equipment; it is particularly a problem if you have the sort of carpet which generates sparks when you touch the door handle. You can buy anti-static spray for the carpet, or an earthed mat that you always touch first.

Dust covers repay their cost many times, as they keep the computer in good condition when not in use, particularly by keeping dust out of the disk drives. Smoking in the room is not a good idea, as the smoke particles can get into the disk drives and cause scratching. Take great care with drinks near the computer: coffee spilt in the keyboard can prove very expensive in repairs, and will not be covered under warranty! Cleaning kits are useful for looking after disks, screens, and other items.

There are a wide range of computer accessories available, which one will find listed in the catalogues of computer supplies firms. Some items such as diskette storage boxes or devices to enable you to remove sprockets holes quickly from listing paper, can be most useful. On the other hand, anti-power-spike devices will usually only duplicate protection that is provided in better quality computers anyway. Other items such as uninterruptible power supplies (to keep things going for a while even in the event of a power cut) and fireproof diskette safes are normally outside the needs of a local church.

An intelligent approach is needed when buying supplies and accessories: certain items can be very useful, but others are very overpriced, and if one gets carried away the total cost of the system will mount up dramatically!

Points for discussion

1. Where would you wish to locate a computer system for your church? Who would have access to it?

2. Do you feel that computer networks and use of data communications offer opportunities relevant to the local church?

3. What priority would you place on ergonomic factors (furniture, environment, etc) in installing a church computer?

6
Getting started _____

Once the hardware and software is chosen, agreement has been reached to place an order, and a suitable location has been found, the church is ready to get started in using the system. Unfortunately, many churches who take great care in the selection of a system make important mistakes at this stage, with the result that the system fails to achieve the benefits that were hoped for, or at best there is a long delay, and possibly additional cost, before much is achieved.

Implementation plans

One of the best ways to avoid such problems is to prepare a clear implementation plan, before the system is received. One cannot expect the computer to meet all the church's needs overnight. An implementation plan will allow it to be brought into use in a systematic way.

This requires commitment: in the short term it may mean committing valuable time to getting work established on the computer, in order for the system to save time in the longer term.

Many churches take up to a year before they begin to get full benefit from their system. Sometimes this is due to lack of planning, but certainly one should allow several months for the implementation period.

The main tasks during this time are:

- installing the computer in the chosen location
- learning to use the system
- entering data into computer files
- establishing procedures for practical use (backups etc).

Each of these is discussed further, either here or in later chapters.

An implementation plan takes these factors into account, and has specific dates for specific applications to be fully operational. It must then be a high priority to make time available for everybody concerned so that these tasks can take place on schedule.

The plan only requires a single page, but may look something like

---

ST JOHN'S, UPPERTON – COMPUTER IMPLEMENTATION PLAN

Stages to be completed by end of months shown.

April 90	Working party to complete decision on choice of systems and prepare report for church council.
May 90	Decision to be taken by church council. Orders for hardware and software to be placed at end of month.
June 90	System due to be received. Initial setup and training in use of hardware etc.
July 90	AB (computer co-ordinator) to be familiar with basic operation of machine and principles of membership system. CD to attend software course with supplier.
August 90	CD and EF (computer assistants) to be trained in use of membership system. CD to have all church members entered by end of August. EF to begin exploring word processing package.
September 90	*Membership system* should be fully operational by now as regards *church members*. Listings to be available for leaders of organisations. EF now able to word process straightforward minutes and reports.
October 90	Church treasurer to begin familiarisation with accounting system. One month's transactions to be entered as a trial. AB to attend course for computer co-ordinators.
November 90	CD and EF to enter all children and adherents on to membership system. EF should now be fully familiar with word processing and able to take over *church newsletter*.
December 90	*Accounting system* to be fully operational with all headings set up ready for full use from 1 January.
January 91	Minister to begin using membership system to plan *pastoral visiting*.
February 91	Covenants secretary to begin familiarisation with *deeds of covenant* software. Existing covenants to be entered. Full use to begin from new tax year starting 6 April.
March 91	Envelope secretary to set up *planned giving* system. Sidespeople to be trained to record weekly envelopes from April.
April 91	All applications now operational.
June 91	Church council to review progress and receive computer produced *six monthly accounts*.
January 92	First computer produced *full year's accounts* to be issued.
April 92	First computerised *deeds of covenant tax claim*.

the example shown. Where possible, it is good if the implementation plan can be approved by the church council when the decision to buy the system is taken. This serves two functions: those using the system know they have the blessing of the church council to devote time to getting familiar with the applications concerned, and it gives the council some dates against which to measure progress in seeing some results from their investment.

The example is for a church that wishes to use some four or five different applications, phased in very gradually over a year or more to suit the various dates of the different church functions. Obviously it may be revised as things proceed – people may learn much more quickly than expected – but it is much better to revise it that way than to have to delay things because problems arose or because people were unable to find the time needed.

Learning to use the system

Although personal computers are relatively straightforward to learn to use – certainly much simpler than learning to drive a car for example – it will take a little while to become familiar with the use of a machine and its software, particularly in knowing what to do if things go wrong.

Essentially there are three distinct areas where users will need to gain expertise:

- the operation of the *hardware*: how to switch on, use the keyboard, insert diskettes, load paper into the printer, change ribbons, cleaning, etc

- general principles of managing software on the given computer: how to format new diskettes, check the directory of files on a disk, copy a file from one disk to another, make backup copies of a disk; in other words, using the computer's *operating system*

- use of the *application software* – the programs that were actually the reason for buying the system; typically there will be several packages to be learned individually, though not all users will need to learn each one.

Usually the computer will have been purchased for at least a couple of different applications – word processing and membership records for example. There is much to be said for getting reasonably familiar with one application before getting involved in others: one cannot learn everything at once.

A user friendly membership application may be a good deal

simpler to start with than word processing, because the former may be entirely *menu-driven*, which means you simply select from lists of options and key in specific information where indicated. Word processing needs knowledge of special key combinations to edit a document, and may require some understanding of the printer if one wishes to produce documents with different typefaces. (On the other hand, if it is desired to use word processing mainly for straightforward letters and reports, and the membership records are being done with software that requires a lot of setting up, it may be easier to start with word processing.)

Training and manuals

As regards training, it is first essential to decide *who* is to do what, so the church can arrange to train the right people (see below under *Personnel*). Several churches have found their computers took a long time to be effective, because those involved initially were unable to take on longer term responsibility for the system. As a result those who actually had to make use of the machine were struggling without the benefit of initial guidance from suppliers.

Keyboard skills need to be considered. It is not necessary to be a trained typist to use a computer; in fact the ease with which corrections can be made means that those whose typing is abysmal can produce excellent results when a computer is used. But a user who has no typing ability at all, not even at the one fingered level, will require extra training time to get used to the layout of keys on a keyboard.

If one plans to use the computer extensively, it is worth attempting to acquire a reasonable keyboard speed, particularly for applications such as word processing where a good deal of text is to be entered. A number of typing tutor software packages are available to assist in this way, and they are much more fun than learning skills with a typing book and a manual typewriter! However, it must be stressed that good keyboard skills are an optional extra, and no one should be put off using the system because of lack of keyboard expertise. All that is needed is the ability to find keys with a one or two fingered approach, and this is in fact what the majority of computer users do.

If the church is buying a system on a fully supported basis, the dealer's staff will probably unpack the hardware and connect it up. They may also give some initial training in the general use of the machine – though this is becoming rarer as hardware gets cheaper. In some cases the dealer may be able to give some initial guidance on the applications software, too – particularly the general purpose packages – but naturally a dealer will not normally have any detailed understanding of church-specific software. Where an initial training day (or even a couple of hours) is being provided, it must be used carefully. It will of necessity be only an introduction, and one must be prepared to follow it up by study of the manuals, but points learned on a training day are very helpful to get started, especially if careful notes are made. It is best to have only one or at most two people present at such initial sessions. They will then establish how the system is to be used in the church, and will take responsibility for training others.

Most of the detailed familiarisation with the system will, however, come from study of the manuals provided, and with lower cost hardware, everything must be learned this way, unless a consultant is being used to give individual support. (That is why the quality of the manuals is such an important consideration in selecting software and hardware.)

There will probably be quite a few manuals: typically a hardware manual for the computer and another for the printer (though a large part of the printer manual is usually control codes, which are only required for very technical word processing). There will be a manual for the operating system (often bound in with the computer hardware manual) and also a manual for each application package to be used. There may be more than one manual for some applications: an introduction or tutorial, and a detailed guide for later use. There may also be some manuals that can be ignored altogether: for example, if the computer has the BASIC programming language, there will usually be a BASIC manual, but put this in a bottom drawer unless you plan to write your own programs. There may also be some reference cards which summarise information likely to be needed quickly, but they are only for use once the principles of the software to which they relate are fully understood.

Having identified the relevant manuals (or the relevant sections if they are bound together) it is essential to learn one's way around them: what to find where. Whoever is to be the main system user – the computer co-ordinator – must then set aside time to read them, at least as far as the introductory chapters and a survey of the remaining material.

Reading the manuals pays more dividends than any other preparation. Surveys show that users who have taken the trouble to study the manuals are invariably more satisfied with their systems, because they are able to make better use of them.

Manuals do not convey only the bare essentials: users will also learn of the numerous facilities which software writers have provided in their packages to allow them to be used for tasks beyond those the church had originally considered.

If funds are available, it is possible to undertake external training courses in the use of certain software, and the dealer or software supplier may have details. It may also be possible to arrange additional one-to-one training; this can be particularly helpful as a review, some months after initial installation.

Training needs to be planned carefully in relation to the various users. Certain applications, such as church accounts or deeds of covenant need to be understood only by one or two people who will use them. On the other hand, the basic operation of the machine, how to format a new diskette and how to get into an application, is something that all users need to know.

It worth trying to ensure that all important details are understood by at least two people. Certainly a password should never be known by one person alone; it should always be recorded in a safe place (perhaps in a sealed envelope) so that in an emergency another person can take over.

Entry of data

For applications that require data to be stored in computer files, it will be necessary to convert church manual records into computer form before the computer system can be of service. In practical terms, this will require someone to key in the relevant information.

A church membership system, for example, requires someone to enter the details of all current church members. Only then can it be used as a basis for producing directories and lists, and to enter new members as they occur.

If the manual records are complete and simply need keying in, it may be quite simple. But very often the current information is incomplete and further details must be researched before it can be entered. Postcodes and telephone numbers may be missing in certain cases. Children may be known in some instances and not others. Quite commonly, members' ages are to be held on the computer (at least approximately) and the minister – or someone who knows almost everyone – must be asked to provide an indication. One may also wish to classify people into areas or housegroups: if so, codes must be allocated for each group and the list of members annotated accordingly.

In a large church, the actual entry of data may be several days work. However, such data entry is usually quite straightforward once the principle is established, and a volunteer may well be able to assist, even if he or she would not have the skills or time to be involved with longer term use of the system. Good keyboard skills are very useful here for cutting down the time.

It is vital that the person entering the information knows *exactly* what is required. Is the first Christian name to be entered, or more? If only initials are known, are full stops to be used? Where should the social title (*Mr*, *Mrs*, etc) be placed? How should the postcode be entered? If two people have the same address, how does one indicate that the second is the same as the one before? What if the address has too many or too few lines? When are capitals required? Are commas to be used at the end of lines? How can information be corrected if it is entered wrongly initially?

If the church wants the information that the system produces to appear in a presentable form, it is well worth giving attention to all these points. Changing a large amount of information at a later date is very time consuming. It is at the data entry stage that it is most important to remember the golden computer rule: *garbage in, garbage out!* Where the software comes with demonstration files, these may be very helpful in deciding the best way to enter the information.

It is very important to consider the arrangements for backup while the data is being entered (see chapter 8) or one can easily lose several days work! It is a good idea to take a backup at least twice a day, during the data entry stage.

Personnel

Establishing who is to do what with the computer is absolutely crucial in allowing the system to have an effective role in church life. Often, churches see the installation of a computer as an opportunity to involve new lay people, but this does require care. If the computer is to be performing tasks that are central to church life, the main users of the system must not only be very committed to the church, but must also be sufficiently involved to make intelligent decisions.

Of greatest importance is to appoint one person to act as a *computer co-ordinator* (or a similar title of the church's choosing). This person will be the chief user, who will provide guidance to all others who use the system, and indicate who is allowed to do what. If there are three or four people using a system with no collaboration it will soon get wrecked, and people will be destroying other people's work.

If the computer has been bought largely for the minister's personal use, then he or she will obviously be the co-ordinator: if anyone else uses the system it will be under the minister's direction. In churches with a full time administrator, that person will usually be the computer co-ordinator. In other cases it may be the church secretary, the minister's secretary, or a specially appointed person.

The responsibilities of the computer co-ordinator include the following tasks:

- overall control of the system: where it is sited, who can use it, whether it may be moved, etc

- allocation of diskettes, and times for use of the machine

- acting as 'local expert' in being the point of reference for others with problems or queries. It follows that the co-ordinator *must* read all the relevant manuals thoroughly, and know exactly where to go to resolve questions. He or she must also be fairly easily available at the times when the system will be in use

- control of the data on the system. This applies primarily to applications such as membership systems where substantial records are kept. The co-ordinator will define who is allowed to access the information for inquiry (checking details, producing listings, etc) and who is allowed to amend information or enter new names. Where the application is controlled by passwords, the co-ordinator will assign passwords and communicate them to the appropriate people. He or she will also set the rules as to how the information is entered (see above under *Entry of data*)

- ensuring that appropriate backup procedures are carried out on a regular basis, in accordance with church requirements

- checking the current levels, and re-ordering supplies (diskettes, paper, printer ribbons) in good time

- registration under the Data Protection Act (see chapter 7) and ensuring that all users of the system comply with the Act. This includes making sure that computer listings are not passed to outside bodies unless covered by the registration, and checking that users do not use free-format 'notes' fields to record inappropriate information about people

- liaising with suppliers. The co-ordinator should act as the contact between suppliers of hardware and software and the users of the system. Suppliers need a named contact to whom technical updates and other information should be sent. If, for example, the church receives notification that a new level of software has been released for a package being used – perhaps to correct a fault – the co-ordinator must arrange to get this and apply it, and inform any other users who may be affected

- resolving hardware and software problems. If anyone experiences a serious problem with the equipment or the software, the co-ordinator will be responsible for contacting the maintenance company or software supplier, or will make arrangements to return the machine for repair. Others who may be dependent on the system must be informed accordingly. It is important that contact with suppliers in such cases is channelled through one person; if everyone rings up the supplier when a problem is suspected it can cause a lot of bad feeling, not to mention practical difficulties in knowing what is happening

- it follows that the co-ordinator must have authority to spend modest amounts of money on ordering supplies, authorising maintenance (if not under contract), purchase of accessories, etc. This must not be left until too late: the co-ordinator must know what authority he or she has in this respect.

Some churches have appointed a computer professional who is a church member to take the co-ordinator role. However, unless this person is actually going to be a regular day to day user, entering data and so on, this is not usually helpful. Such a person is unlikely to be able to fulfil many of the duties at all effectively: a non-technical person who is actually using the system most of the time and who is given the appropriate authority is in a better position. Nevertheless, it can be very useful if the co-ordinator has a computer person in the church to whom he or she can turn for technical help, without having to contact suppliers every time.

In addition to the co-ordinator there will typically be a number of *application users* who work with specific packages. These users will need to learn only the basic hardware usage, and the operation of their own application. For example, the church council secretary and the minister may use the membership system, the minister's secretary may use word processing, and the treasurer may use a spreadsheet for financial planning. It is worth avoiding too many users: up to about five is reasonable, with a maximum of three involved in any one application.

It is important that each user is aware of the responsibility of the computer co-ordinator, and knows to turn to the co-ordinator in case of problems. If the applications are quite separate it is a good idea for users to have their own diskettes (or their own sub-directories on a hard disk machine).

It is helpful if one of the users can be the *deputy computer co-ordinator*, with authority to act for the co-ordinator when the latter is on holiday or unavailable. Appointing a deputy (who must be properly briefed by the main co-ordinator) also reduces the risk of vital information (such as passwords, suppliers' telephone numbers, or methods of taking backups) being lost in the event of the co-ordinator meeting with an accident. Remember that if the computer is effectively used in the church, losing the co-ordinator can be as serious as losing the minister!

Effective use of the system

Once consideration has been given to all the issues above, and a suitable implementation plan has been put into effect, it is important to get to the point where the computer is a dependable tool in church life.

A sensible change from existing methods of working is naturally required. Where a task previously undertaken by hand is to be transferred to computer there is much to be said for a period of *parallel running* during which the old and the new procedures are carried out simultaneously and compared: this is especially useful in financial applications where one needs to be sure of the computer produced figures. So it is not a good idea to dispose of all the paper records as soon as they are entered on the computer.

But equally, there comes a point, once a system has been proven, when the computer must be regarded as the central record of information. For example, if church membership is to be held on computer, the computer record must be considered definitive, and any paper records required will be the result of computer produced listings.

Reaching this stage of confidence is vital if the computer is to play a full part in church life. It requires a commitment to accurate entry of data, to keeping that data up to date, to making arrangements for maintenance and backup sufficient to avoid serious difficulties even in the event of system faults (see chapter 8) and to effective training of those who use the system. But, once achieved, the contribution of the system to church life may be very substantial indeed.

Points for discussion

1. Prepare a possible implementation plan for a system to be installed in your church. Pay particular attention to the training arrangements.

2. Who would be the most suitable person in your church to act as computer co-ordinator? How would you enable someone to acquire the skills needed?

3. A few churches buy computers but never really get round to making effective use of them. Why do you think this is? How would you ensure this did not happen in your own church?

7
Ethical issues and data protection ____

Most computer applications in churches require some information about individuals to be held on computer. In many cases, the information is exactly the same as would be kept by manual means if the church had no computer. But because computer held information can be processed and analysed much more quickly than manual records, there are sometimes concerns about possible abuse of that information.

For this reason, the law provides restrictions on the use of personal information on computers, and Christians will likewise wish to maintain clear ethical guidelines in determining how computer held information is used. There is a strong Christian tradition of the confidentiality of communications between priest and parishioner or between pastor and church member – the privacy of the confessional or the counselling room – and this must not be broken in any way by the use of computers.

There is rarely a problem here, as few ministers would commit highly confidential information to paper, still less put it on computer. It is important to reassure those who may be concerned that only clear factual information will be held on the system. However, it is impossible to computerise areas such as membership records or deeds of covenant without keeping certain confidential information about individuals or families on the system, and this is where care is needed.

Christian attitudes to use of information

In practice, there are two main ethical issues to resolve:

- what information is to be held about people?
- who may have access to that information?

All those who hold personal data (i.e. data about living people) on computer must take account of the Data Protection Act, as described below. The process of deciding how to register under the Act will require the church to determine its answers to the questions posed above.

Deciding *what* information to hold is largely determined by the software. For example, any software package to manage deeds of covenant will require the covenantor's name, the date of the deed, the annual amount, and so on. A membership system may allow a wider choice, but the concept is similar. It is with free format fields for notes or codes that the greatest care must be taken. For example, a user wishing to be helpful might add a note about a boy/girl friendship, which in effect meant that details were being held about members' sexual behaviour! This could justifiably cause concern.

Deciding about *access* to information is often harder. Anyone who might ever receive a printout has effectively had access to church records, and a clear church policy is needed to decide what can be disclosed to whom. For example, names and addresses will normally be available to all church members, but pastoral information will normally be available only to the minister or others in pastoral charge. Financial information about covenants will have to be available to the covenants secretary and to the Inland Revenue, but will probably be kept confidential from the minister and other church members.

It is also important that anyone can have access to their own information. In most situations this will be required under the Data Protection Act in any case, but even without this it could be very destructive to keep information and refuse to allow a member to see what was held about them. Openness with individuals about their own information is bound to lead to greater confidence in the use of the computer within the church.

The Data Protection Act provides a convenient framework for thinking about all these issues, and must serve as a minimum requirement. Many churches will, however, wish to go further than the Act requires, perhaps by including manual records in their consideration, or perhaps by taking rather stricter measures in managing church information than is actually required by the Act.

Churches are now used to the stewardship of money, the

stewardship of buildings, and the stewardship of people's time and abilities, but increasingly we must think too about the stewardship of information. Often the information in the church's possession is one of its most precious assets (certainly in spiritual terms this will almost always be so) and the appropriate care and use of that information is important.

To many churches this is a new way of thinking, and it opens up ethical questions which are well outside what many members can handle. If so, decisions may have to be taken by a small number of people who understand the implications. But failing to consider questions surrounding the use of information in the church can amount to negligence in the management of church resources, and can have quite serious effects on people's lives.

It is impossible to set a blueprint for all churches. Some will wish to be very open, and members will be happy to allow other members to know almost anything about them. Some may even be willing for the list of members' names and addresses to be available to the general public. At the other end of the scale are churches where even telephone numbers are kept ex-directory and not normally disclosed to members other than personal friends.

Once such decisions are made, it is possible to proceed to a registration under the Data Protection Act, and the remainder of this chapter deals with that Act insofar as it affects churches.

The discussion that follows is based on information current at the time of writing, and amendments, orders by the Secretary of State, or decisions of the courts, could cause the details to change. It should, therefore not be taken as an authoritative statement of the law, but as general guidance.

The Data Protection Act

In 1984 the Data Protection Act became law in the United Kingdom. This was the first occasion that a major piece of legislation had been passed relating specifically to computer systems and their use. The Act is of interest to churches both from a moral point of view, and from a practical point of view in relation to computers used in the church.

For the most part, Christians will welcome such legislation, in that it is concerned with protecting the individual, although in some respects one might wish it went further.

It has long been recognised that, whenever records are kept about people or their activities, there are dangers of abuse. The Act distinguishes data users (those who maintain computer files and use the information in them) from data subjects (those whose details are recorded in the files). The legislation is largely about balancing the needs and the rights of data subjects and data users. (There is also a third party – the computer bureau – which may handle information even though it is not the data user. Churches and individual ministers may not regard themselves as computer bureaux, but if they keep files for anyone else, they probably are. Further details are given in the final section of this chapter.)

The Act is concerned with personal data; there are no restrictions on keeping data that has nothing to do with people, such as lists of biblical references. But the data does not have to be highly sensitive to be personal; lists of names and addresses count as personal data for most purposes. Statistical data is excluded provided anything identifying individuals has been removed.

The Act relates only to data processed by computer, so manual files are exempt, which is one of the criticisms of the Act, but even the smallest home computer can process data automatically, and so the data is subject to the Act. Word processing as such does not count, but clearly if word processed material is kept for longer term reference, the data in the documents is being used for other purposes too.

The Act is entirely concerned with protection of *data*. The Data Protection Act is not concerned with the issues of protecting *programs* from unauthorised copying; this is the subject of a quite separate Act – see under *Software licensing* in chapter 3.

Data Protection Principles

The basis of the legislation is a list of Data Protection Principles* which are to be observed by all data users:

1. *The information to be contained in personal data shall be obtained, and personal data shall be processed, fairly and lawfully.* (So you cannot set up files of information obtained by deceit.)

2. *Personal data shall be held only for one or more specified and lawful purposes.* (So you cannot keep personal data just because you feel like it – there must be a specific purpose.)

3. *Personal data held for any purpose or purposes shall not be used or disclosed in any manner incompatible with that purpose or those purposes.* (So you cannot get people's names for the purpose of putting them on an electoral roll, but use the list for selling double glazing.)

*Data Protection Act 1984, Schedule 1.

4. *Personal data held for any purpose or purposes shall be adequate, relevant, and not excessive in relation to that purpose or those purposes.* (So you must not hold lots of juicy facts about people – even if they are true – unless they are relevant to the specified purpose of holding the data in the first place.)

5. *Personal data shall be accurate and, where necessary, kept up to date.* (So if you keep any data, you must do it properly. Be certain that you have the resources to keep it up to date when details change.)

6. *Personal data held for any purpose or purposes shall not be kept for longer than is necessary for that purpose or purposes.* (So you must remove personal data about parishioners no longer under your care unless there is a definite reason why it needs to be retained.)

7. *An individual shall be entitled –*
   (a) *at reasonable intervals and without undue delay or expense*
      (i) *to be informed by any data user whether he holds personal data of which that individual is the subject; and*
      (ii) *to access to any such data held by a data user; and*
   (b) *where appropriate, to have such data corrected or erased.* (So you must have the means to make data available and correct it as required.)

8. *Appropriate security measures shall be taken against unauthorised access to, or alteration of, personal data and against accidental loss or destruction of personal data.* (So you must prevent unauthorised access to files of personal data, and have a good system of backups to stop data being lost in the event of any failures.)

Most of these principles seem ethically very reasonable. They stop people keeping data, and then abusing that right by disclosing confidential details that should be kept private, and they stop data being kept about us without our knowledge.

The practical way the Act implements these principles is through the Data Protection Registrar, with whom data must be registered, and who has powers to stop certain abuses by serving enforcement notices, or prosecuting offenders. The Registrar is appointed by the Crown, and works with a staff of around 30 from offices in Wilmslow, Cheshire.

The various requirements of the Act came into force at different dates, and these are described below.

Safeguarding data

The requirement to take care of data and avoid damaging disclosures came into force on 12 September 1984. All personal data that a church holds should be properly protected, by physical security (keeping the diskettes locked up) and/or by software protection through passwords etc. Users must not pass on mailing lists etc without the permission of the people whose names are held.

This is fairly straightforward to comply with. The most common breach of this in church life is with people who are anxious to demonstrate their computer systems to others, and in doing so, disclose details about real people. If one gives demonstrations, one must set up fictitious data. Users of the system must also, of course, destroy any unwanted listings that contain personal data.

Registration

The second main requirement of the Act is that all data users – which will include virtually all users of computers in church work – must register with the Data Protection Registrar. Since 11 May 1986 it has been illegal to process personal data by computer without being registered. Anyone who uses personal data in any way other than as specified in their registration, will be guilty of an offence, and could be liable to a large fine and confiscation of their data. In the case of corporate bodies (such as churches) both the body and the individuals responsible for the data can be punished; you cannot be excused on the grounds that your church council never told you to register.

The Register is open to public inspection (copies are being held by main libraries, for example) so anyone can discover what sort of information a given church is holding, where they get it from and who they pass it on to.

For churches, it will be membership type lists that are most likely to give a need to register, as they will necessarily contain personal data. Financial information will also need to be registered if it relates to individuals, for example in planned giving schemes or deeds of covenant records.

Registration involves completing forms (obtainable free in Post Offices or direct from the Registrar) and forwarding them with the registration fee (£40 from November 1987) to the Registrar. The forms are in two sections: Part A is for details about the data user who is registering and Part B is for details of the data and its uses.

A separate Part B is completed for each *purpose* for which personal data is held; generally a purpose will correspond to an application. The forms provide a large number of standard categories that can simply be selected by ticking boxes: popular purposes for processing personal data in churches will include *P010 Membership Administra-*

tion and *P005 Fund Raising* amongst others. The remaining information requested on each part B comes under four headings.

The first heading asks for details of the *data subjects* about whom information is held by the church. Category *S016 Members and Supporters* will usually be relevant, though some churches will need to include other categories too. One also indicates for each category whether it relates to current, past, or potential subjects, so by ticking the *potential* heading against the *Members* category one is allowing for outreach work to those who may become members of the church at a future date. It is best to avoid the catch-all category *Members of the Public* unless the church really does keep data on all parishioners, as the Registrar is rightfully very uneasy about users who may keep data on anyone at all.

Under the second heading one describes the *classes* of data held about people. Classes that will be useful to churches include *C001 Personal identifiers* (this includes name, address, telephone number); *C011 Personal details* (age, sex, date of birth); *C037 Membership of voluntary or charitable bodies* (this includes offices held); and so on. Each church must, however, consider the classes very carefully, as needs will vary greatly from church to church: some churches wish to keep much more comprehensive information than others. The Registrar offers around 60 standard classes to choose from, and those with appropriate responsibility in the church need to sit down and decide very carefully what information the church may or may not ever wish to record. It is not a decision that can be taken by computer specialists: those in pastoral work need to be actively involved. A lot depends on considering what sort of free format notes one might have on file. *C123 Religious beliefs* will usually be needed if baptism and confirmation details are kept; it may also be necessary to include classes such as *C111 Physical health record* or *C113 Disabilities or infirmities* if comments about illnesses are sometimes recorded in the notes.

The third heading on the Part B relates to *sources* and *disclosures*: where the information is obtained from, and whom it is passed to. The general rule is to be liberal with sources (so that data obtained from any relevant body can be recorded) but restrictive with disclosures (since personal data should not be passed on to any more people.than absolutely necessary). This again will vary from church to church. Where information is kept by a minister purely for his or her own use, there will be no disclosures at all. Usually, however, most of the information will be available to *D201 Members* and to *D110 Spiritual and advice workers*, for example. It is easy to overlook the headings related to government departments, but a covenants system must, of course, include disclosure *D301 Inland Revenue;*

churches who operate schools will also need *D321 Local Government Education Department.*

It is also a very good idea to include disclosure *D206 Suppliers and providers of goods and services* on all Part Bs; this means that if a major problem occurs with an application, the file can legitimately be passed to the software supplier for investigation. Experience suggests that users occasionally make mistakes with systems which cause membership files to be corrupted, and sometimes the technical expertise of the software house enables the problem to be rectified without the entire file having to be re-keyed. However, an appropriate disclosure must be registered to allow this.

The fourth heading relates to *overseas transfers* of data. This is unlikely to affect many churches except perhaps one or two involved in exchange of detailed information with missionaries.

There is something to be said for submitting more than one Part B for a single purpose in order to clarify what information is kept and disclosed to whom. For example, it may be that quite detailed information is held about church members, but that much less is kept on other categories of people. Similarly, names and addresses may be disclosed quite widely, but more sensitive information may be kept on a quite restrictive basis: if this is put entirely on one Part B it can suggest, to anyone inspecting the Register, that the church is keeping confidential information on all and sundry and disclosing it far and wide. Someone hostile to the church could, for example, create very bad publicity by giving lurid examples of what the church was legally entitled to do under its registration, if there were just a single very broad Part B.

One has to re-register every three years. In the meantime, if any of the details change (such as if a new application is started, or if the user's address changes) the registration must be amended. It is worth trying to allow for likely future uses when registering initially. The Registrar has the power to disallow registered uses that are too open ended or which would contravene the Data Protection Principles.

There are certain exemptions from registration, which include data held for national security, data used only for payrolls and accounts (but not if one has any non-accounting data in them), data used only for domestic or recreational purposes (so one's Christmas card list need not be registered, but one cannot argue that church files are only recreational), and name and address lists used only for distributing literature, provided the people concerned have agreed to the data being held. Some churches who keep computer lists purely for distributing newsletters, where the list is never used for anything else, may be able to fit in this exemption, but such an approach offers little hope of the computer as a serious church tool.

There is also an exemption from registration for unincorporated members' clubs if data is only held about members, provided they have agreed. It is possible that a few independent free churches could regard themselves as clubs, to get round this, but this would not apply in the main denominations. However, this exemption cannot be used if one needs to hold data on any non-members or without getting the permission of all who are members, so it may be easier to register anyway.

Even if the church were exempt from registration, it would still have to observe the Data Protection Principles. Moreover, the requirement to get permission of every person is very restrictive. If a person objects, that person has to be excluded from computer lists, or else one has to make their consent a condition of church membership, and exclude those who will not comply. One of the big advantages of registering is that everything done in accordance with that registration is automatically legal; one doesn't need every individual to agree.

Thus, the general rule must certainly be: if in doubt register. Apart from anything else, it proves the church's concern to comply with the Act, and it avoids the risk of penalties if it is required to register.

It is worth giving a lot of thought to the nature of the registration, both so that one does not have to keep changing it, and to ensure that it properly covers all the personal data the church plans to hold on the computer and the uses to which it will be put. In most cases the registration will be in the name of the church as the data user, specifying perhaps the minister's address as the correspondence address for data subjects. On that basis, it should be unnecessary for the church to re-register if there should be a change of minister or any lay officers. But where clergy have bought computer systems personally, and are using them without any direction from the church, then the minister as an individual would be the data user, and would have to register.

The Act requires the registration to be made by the *legal entity* which controls that data: if there are distinct legal entities (e.g. separate trusts or limited companies) they must register separately. The location of the legal entity varies by denomination: it may be at the (equivalent of) parish, diocese, or whole denomination.

Anglican churches will thus often have to submit two registrations (frequently identical), one in the name of the incumbent and the other in the name of the parochial church council, although it is sometimes possible to argue that the data is controlled entirely by one or the other. By contrast, the Methodist Church has made a single registration for the whole denomination, though a system of internal registration ensures that local churches stay within its terms.

Diocesan advisers and the like will want to keep a careful eye, to ensure that the church is not brought into disrepute by individual churches failing to fulfil their Data Protection Act obligations.

Subject access

The third stage, effective from 11 November 1987, requires that all data users must be able to inform anyone who requests it whether they hold data about that person, and if so what it is. One can charge up to £10 if desired (though this may not help congregational rapport!) and one has 40 days to supply the details, but they must not be deliberately changed in the meantime.

The information must be in a form that the data subject can understand, so users who have lots of codes or unidentified fields must give explanation of what they mean. It is most important to give all the information one holds – even if it is spread over several files – and one cannot leave out confidential bits, even if they are only matters of opinion. (The church can, however, leave out details of future intentions such as 'it is intended to excommunicate this person'!)

Any software must therefore have the ability to print out the details about one person. Moreover, the subject must only receive details on him or herself, not anyone else. (This is clearly a problem if data is kept by families.)

There are a number of exemptions from this right of subject access. (These are distinct from the exemptions from registration: one may be required to register, but may be entitled to refuse subject access.) The main exemption is criminal records, and the Home Secretary also has powers to exempt medical information (including mental health) and certain data held for social work.

Even if the Home Secretary decides to exercise these powers, it is not clear whether pastoral data held by clergy could fall in these categories. However, it would seem in the best interests of pastoral relationships to allow individuals to see any data held about them. This implies that users will take care in the recording of data in the first place.

If a data subject points out (with reasonable evidence) that any data the church holds is incorrect, it must be corrected or the record must be deleted altogether.

It is, of course, vital to ensure that subject access requests do in fact come from the subject and not from someone else trying to find out about them! Churches would be well advised to insist on requests being written and signed, or made in person if the individual is known. It would also be unwise to agree to post a copy of the subject's information to any address other than their own. There should also be a rule that only the computer co-ordinator (or appointed deputy) is allowed to respond to subject access requests.

From the point of view of enabling those in church life to avoid worries about the uses of church computer systems, there is much to be said for being as flexible as possible in allowing subject access, but one does not legally *have to* unless:

- the request is received in writing at the address specified in the data protection registration

- whatever fee the church requires is paid (subject to a £10 maximum)

- the request is received on or after 11 November 1987.

The church can also ask for supplementary information needed to trace data subjects. For example, if data is only kept on those who have attended church, one could ask the subject whether he or she had ever attended any of the churches covered by the registration, and if so, which, so that the relevant file can be checked. This is likely to be useful where several churches are registered as a single entity, to avoid having to check every file each time a subject access request is received. If one wished to be particularly difficult, it is possible to submit several separate registrations under the Act (this may be helpful if the church has several computers for different purposes controlled by different people); the data subject would then have to submit a request and payment in respect of every one separately. But such approaches are contrary to the spirit of the law, and represent a very un-Christian attitude. Pastoral concern requires the greatest possible co-operation in assisting those who wish to see what data is held about them.

Software requirements

In summary, to comply with the Act, all software used to store personal data must have the ability:

- to control access to the data in the first place, e.g. by use of passwords

- to separate the data concerning each person

- to produce a printed copy of that data in a fairly readable form

- to provide demonstrations by means of a separate file of fictitious data.

The overall effect

Data protection is a serious issue that many microcomputer users assume relates only to firms with large mainframes. But in general the principles should be welcomed by Christians, and being expected to comply with them is not unreasonable and is in everyone's interest.

The general approach is based on an encouragement of openness about the use of computer systems, but coupled with a strict obligation to protect the confidentiality of data about each individual.

If the church is aware of the issues, plans carefully the reasons for the data to be held, registers appropriately, keeps live data confidential, and only uses software with the necessary requirements, there should be few problems.

Other people's data

Any person or organisation which processes any data for other people or which allows others to use its equipment for storing personal data, is considered to be operating a *computer bureau* for the purposes of the Data Protection Act. If for example another church keeps files on your computer, you are regarded as a computer bureau, and must comply with the specific requirements of the Act in that area.

There is no particular problem in this. When registering your own data, it is simply necessary to register as a *data user who is also a computer bureau*. This merely involves ticking a different box; there is no extra charge.

As a bureau, you would be responsible for complying with the eighth Data Protection Principle (about ensuring appropriate security of personal data), but the others are the responsibility of the data user.

However, the data user must also submit their own registration – they are still responsible for personal data processed by computer – even though the computer is not in their possession. They will also be responsible for fulfilling subject access requirements, and the service that you provide to them by way of hardware, software, etc must enable them to do this. (Typically the data user will say to you: "I have received a subject access request from a Fred Bloggs of this address. Please would you check whether we hold any information about him, and if so, provide me with a print of that information so we can forward it to him.") If you just provide the hardware for them to use, they will do this themselves.

However, a church would be well advised to avoid acting as a computer bureau for anyone using personal data, unless it is confident that this service can be provided. In particular, note the 40 day limit for subject requests; if the person in charge of the computer tends to go on six week holidays, or if your equipment is ever out of order for this period, you could be in difficulties!

The fundamental issue as to whether you are the data user or just a computer bureau depends on whether or not the data is under your control. If you, as a church, also process data for another church, then you are almost certainly a bureau, even if they simply use your hardware with no involvement from yourself. If anyone using your system keeps personal data on it, you must still register under the Act, as a bureau, even if you have no personal data of your own. However, the Registrar has indicated that an individual who is using his or her own computer for church work, would not need to register as a bureau, provided the church is registered and the individual is clearly an officer of the church in some way.

Points for discussion

1. What Christian obligations exist in the 'stewardship of information'?

2. To what extent should church information be available to others? Consider several different types of information, e.g. names, addresses, telephone numbers, ages, dates when pastoral visits were received, value of covenants, illnesses/disabilities etc.

3. Would you wish to extend the notion of subject access to information *not* held on computer? Or do you feel ministers should be allowed to keep confidential records about parishioners which are not open to the individuals concerned?

8
Avoiding problems ⎯⎯⎯⎯⎯⎯⎯

There is no such thing as a perfect computer system which will never go wrong, just as there is no such person as a user who will never make a mistake. This limitation is true of almost all tools: cars are a frequent course of problems, though few would do without them merely because of that. Even the humble spade used to till the soil may break in two, and arrangements must be made for its repair or replacement.

It should be said that there is very little chance of a computer making a mistake – the nature of the electronics makes the probability of error infinitesimally small. Bugs in the software could cause wrong results to be produced, but if the software is well proven the chances of this are also fairly low. Most mistakes in results are likely to be due to human errors when information was input: garbage in, garbage out.

However, there is always a small, but not insignificant, chance that the computer might break down and produce no information at all (until repaired). There is also a chance that a hardware or software fault, or a major user error, could cause information to be lost.

Without proper planning, such problems can defeat even the most committed attempt to apply a computer in church work. Many of the classic disaster stories (where a computer has caused more harm than good) relate to an initial failure to consider what should be done if problems arise. Fortunately, though, it is possible to take appropriate steps so that if problems do occur, the effect can be minimised, and the computer continues to be a useful tool on a long term basis.

The main steps required are to make arrangements for maintenance and support according to the church's needs, and to take ample backups of all information, to guard against loss. If this is done it is likely that most people in the church, apart from those directly operating the computer, would never be aware if a fault had occurred.

Backup of data

Successful use of a computer system requires recognition that any information stored is essentially 'fragile', and can be lost if proper precautions are not taken.

Anything recorded on a diskette, whether programs or data, *could* be lost due to any of the following:

- a power failure while the diskette is in the computer

- the diskette being physically damaged, e.g. coffee spilt or placed on a hot radiator

- a user error, such as accidentally deleting the wrong file or reformatting a disk with important data on it or taking a diskette out without terminating the program

- the diskette physically wearing out after considerable use

- a hardware fault damaging the disk, e.g. a damaged disk drive head

- excessive magnetic interference such as placing the diskette next to the telephone when it rings

- a major disaster such as fire or flood.

One needs to establish procedures – and educate users – so that all these events are minimised, but they cannot be avoided altogether. This means that *any information of importance, whether programs or data, must always be kept on at least two disks.* Very important data may justify more than two copies.

Fortunately, one of the advantages of a computer is that it is relatively quick and cheap to copy onto a second diskette (unlike duplicate copying of large manual records).

When any software is received, a copy should be made onto a second diskette, and that copy used for day to day work. If anything happens to it, one can always make a new copy from the original diskette.

However, it is with the church's own data that the greatest care must be taken, particularly in large files that have taken a long time to set up. If the church were to lose the computer through a disaster such as fire or theft, one would make an insurance claim and buy a new one, but if the church's own information is lost it is irreplaceable.

Information to be backed up

When creating church membership files, a backup copy should be taken at frequent intervals. How often is up to you, but remember that one could lose all the data on a working disk in the event of a power cut (say). If that happens, the user makes a new working copy from the backup (this is called *restoring*) and must *re-enter all changes made since the backup was taken.* In regular use, one will probably want to take a backup at least once a week, or ideally after every session in which any changes have been entered to the files. The frequency chosen for backups is a matter of balancing the overhead of taking backups against the inconvenience of re-entering all changes since the last backup if a problem does arise. Keep all pieces of paper that were used as prompts to enter changes, at least until the backup is taken, so that if the working copy should be lost, one would be able to re-enter the changes.

With important data such as membership files, it is a good idea to have more than one backup diskette (say X and Y) and backup onto each alternately (i.e. one day you backup onto X, the next day onto Y). Otherwise there is a small risk of losing all the information, including the backup, in the unlikely event of a power failure while you are making the backup, or due to a mistake in recovering from a backup copy. Always note which of X or Y is current. Some people like to have a different backup diskette for each day of the week.

To guard against major disasters a further backup copy is recommended, held in another building – perhaps taken once a month. After all, however many backup copies are taken, if they are all next to the computer, a fire will destroy them all! In considering major disasters it is necessary to include the risk of theft or burglary. If the hardware is taken it is bad enough, but if diskettes are lost too there is a risk of disclosure of confidential information. If burglary is considered a significant risk, diskettes should be locked up at night well away from the computer.

Backup must also be considered for word processed material. The word processor should be instructed to save one's work from time to time (in case of a power failure) and for work of any importance a copy should be taken onto a second diskette. For full scale accounting the need for backup is even more crucial; failures here can lead to wholly incorrect figures.

Methods of backup

The easiest way to take backups on a floppy disk machine (particularly if there are two disk drives) is to use the operating system to copy the whole of the working diskette onto a backup diskette. Alternatively, some software packages have built in backup facilities which may be more convenient.

Hard disk users will use special operating system utility commands that allow them to copy their hard disk files onto floppy diskettes for backup. If a file is too large to fit on a floppy (which is often the case as much of the reason for having a hard disk is to allow larger files) the user taking the backup is prompted to enter subsequent diskettes as required. These diskettes must then be labelled very carefully, because if it is necessary to restore the file from the floppies, following a problem, the complete set of backup diskettes will be needed and they have to be reinserted one by one in the same order as when the backup was taken. Learning how to do this is one of the major factors that adds to the complexity of hard disk machines, but it is vital that hard disk users know how to take backups on this basis.

All files on the hard disk must be backed up in some way, as very occasionally a major hardware fault requires the replacement of the entire hard disk. If this happens, everything on the hard disk must be restored from floppies once a new hard disk is installed. A problem of this magnitude should be exceptionally rare – perhaps once in five years at the outside – but if one is not prepared, the effect can be devastating.

To ease such problems, some hard disk users buy an additional peripheral device known as a *tape streamer*. Although this involves significant extra cost, a tape streamer can copy an entire hard disk on to a small magnetic tape cartridge in a matter of a few minutes, so it is reasonable to do this once a day. (To copy a standard 20 Mb hard disk onto standard 360 kb floppies requires 60 floppies if the hard disk is full, so this is simply not viable on a regular basis. Therefore the majority of hard disk users who do not have tape streamers work simply by backing up the files which have been modified each day, and keeping very careful records so they know which diskettes to use for recreating which files in the event of problems.)

To use a hard disk machine successfully requires considerable extra care in respect of backups, and the computer co-ordinator must ensure this is handled properly.

How much trouble is taken with backups is up to each church to decide, and with good quality equipment used with proper control, the occasions when one will *need* the backup will be very few and far between. A lot depends on how much work one is prepared to do again when something *does* go wrong. A failure to consider the backup issue properly will sooner or later cause major problems in seeking to apply the computer effectively in church life.

Maintenance and support

Although hardware faults are rare if good quality equipment is chosen, a hardware fault will almost certainly occur at some point. Hardware problems are always a cause of frustration, as they inevitably occur when one is trying to do something important (hardware faults are never a problem when the machine is switched off!). However, the frustration and upset to the church can be much reduced with proper plans for dealing with hardware failures.

In the first place, users should do all they can to reduce hardware problems: look after the equipment, keep it clean. Do not allow anyone to smoke near the machine, and preferably not even in the room, whether the machine is on or off, as smoke particles can damage the disk drives. Follow the manufacturer's instructions if the disk drives require regular cleaning. Look after diskettes and *never* touch the diskette surface. Do not allow excessive dust to accumulate in the printer, and replace ribbons before they are too worn. If a problem does occur, eliminate possible software faults; usually the software manuals will give sufficient guidance to allow one to tell if a problem is software related.

Many hardware faults are only detected by a message from the software. For example, a fault on a disk drive will not usually be visible to the user, but if the software habitually reports error messages such as *Disk sector not found* or *Device I/O error*, and these occur with more than one diskette, there is a fairly good chance that the disk drive is at fault.

If a message of this kind occurs only with one diskette, the diskette itself is probably worn or damaged, and it is necessary to restore from the backup copy onto a new diskette. If it is a long time since the last backup was taken, and a lot of information would have to be re-entered, it may be worth trying the diskette in the other drive (if there are two). It may also be worth trying to take a copy of the entire damaged diskette; sometimes the disk copy utility can read the diskette even when an ordinary program cannot. However, do not persist too long, as using a worn or damaged diskette can actually damage the computer's disk drive. If frequent backups are taken, the occasional loss of a diskette should not be too serious, and must be planned for.

Most hardware faults relate to the mechanical parts of the equipment: disk drives, keyboards, printer mechanisms, plugs and connections. Problems may be worse in extremes of temperature. Always identify the faulty item, and have a clear description to give when requesting repair. Sometimes it may be necessary to ring a dealer or supplier for advice in order to know where the fault lies; this is where support becomes important.

Hardware maintenance

In getting hardware faults repaired there are three main approaches, depending on how long the church could manage without the computer in the event of a fault, and on what the church is able to pay.

The first and cheapest option is not to have any maintenance contract at all, but simply to return equipment to the supplier (or distributor nominated by the supplier) in the event of a fault, and pay the applicable repair charge (unless the equipment is still under warranty). Over 50 per cent of churches find this approah acceptable, which means one is not paying out for faults that do not occur, but one must be able to manage without the computer for a reasonable while – certainly a couple of weeks including delivery each way, and possibly longer if the repair centre is busy. Bear in mind that the church could have to meet a large bill if expensive parts have to be replaced, though this is fairly rare. One may also be reluctant to return the machine for faults that do not put it completely out of action, which makes this approach frustrating. For many users with floppy disk machines, this option may be acceptable, but it would be rather a risky option with a hard disk machine. If a problem occurs with the hard disk, the cost can be extremely high as hard disks can only be serviced by being removed to a special laboratory with 'clean room' conditions.

The second option is to take out computer breakdown insurance. This allows one to call out an engineer from any suitable firm (manufacturer or independent) to repair the machine. The hourly rates charged in such cases tend to be extremely high (because firms like to encourage people to take out maintenance contracts) but the insurance company picks up the majority of the charge: the user simply pays an excess. One will be dealt with at a lower priority than customers with maintenance contracts. But this option is usually a good deal quicker than returning a machine, and takes up less of your time, since the engineer will come to you – though one must, of course, have someone available to meet the engineer and discuss the fault (preferably the computer co-ordinator). It also guarantees that once the premium is paid, the church will never have to pay more than the excess when a fault occurs. Most policies also include cover for ordinary loss or damage to the computer, and sometimes a contribution towards the costs of recreating lost data. An attraction for churches is that insurance premiums are currently exempt from VAT. For relatively expensive equipment which is basically reliable, this may be cheaper than a maintenance contract.

The third possible option is to enter into a full maintenance contract whereby a supplier or maintenance firm commits to servicing one's equipment as and when required, for an inclusive annual fee covering parts and labour. In many cases the contract includes a commitment to having an engineer on the user's premises within a certain time, and may even provide for a replacement machine to be loaned if a repair cannot be accomplished within a certain time. The cost is not cheap, because engineers and spares have to be kept available, but if the church plans to rely heavily on the system, and could not manage without it for more than a day or two, this approach is recommended. With the emergence of lower cost hardware, more economical maintenance contracts are becoming available; typical costs are between 8 and 15 per cent of the hardware cost per annum. There is normally a discount on maintenance contracts while equipment is under warranty. Sometimes there is a choice between a maintenance contract from the manufacture or one from an independent firm. The latter is usually a little cheaper, although they will probably not carry the same range of parts, and there are some highly disreputable firms around, so only act on a good personal recommendation.

Note that maintenance is geared to office hours. If the machine breaks down while you are preparing a sermon on Friday evening, you are unlikely to get it repaired before Tuesday, even with a maintenance contract. Also the arrival of the engineer does not guarantee instant resolution of the problem: a part may have to be ordered or if the fault is intermittent the machine may have to be removed for bench testing. And even if the contract includes a replacement machine in such cases, it is often 'subject to availability'.

Whatever approach is chosen, the computer co-ordinator must be sure what to do *before* a fault arises, so that when a problem does occur he or she can immediately ring the chosen engineers or pack up the system for return to the supplier. Do not be afraid to chase if there is no response within the time you expect.

As the church's dependence on the system increases, it needs to review the maintenance arrangements. A new application which uses the computer on a tight weekly timescale may require much more formal maintenance arrangements than previous applications.

One way of easing the maintenance problem is to have two computers, and large churches should consider this seriously as an alternative to one very expensive machine (as discussed in chapter 5). The machines must, of course, be compatible, and it may be necessary to purchase extra copies of software. When both machines are working, two people can be using them, but if one breaks down there will probably be no great panic to get it repaired within a few hours, so long as the second one is available. (This also makes problem diagnosis quite easy: if a problem occurs on one machine but not when the diskette is transferred to the other, it is very likely to be a hardware fault on the first machine.)

The two machine approach is less useful with hard disks, but it may be that some applications such as word processing could continue using a second machine with floppy drives only. With two machines it may be considered acceptable to deal with all faults by returning the hardware for repair, rather than taking out a contract of any kind.

In most cases, the need for hardware maintenance will be rare, but for effective church use one must have some procedure for when a problem arises.

Software maintenance

Maintenance does not only apply to hardware: it must also be considered in relation to software. Software is not subject to wear and tear in the same way as hardware, but there is always the possibility of a previously unknown fault (a bug) coming to light. If problems arise due to either a fault or a user difficulty, the support available becomes very important.

If software is being bought that has been proven by a number of other churches, the likelihood of faults is small, but there is always a possibility that one may use some previously untried combination of functions which fails to work correctly. Such faults should be reported to the software supplier for rectification, but software houses operate various practices when faults are reported.

A significant amount of software is sold 'as is' with no guarantees, and it is entirely up to the developer whether to take any action at all. Better packages will be guaranteed, but as suppliers develop them new versions may come along, and the church must be prepared to purchase these (if chargeable) to continue the service. Other packages may include an initial free support period, and after that there is an annual charge for support, similar to hardware.

One problem with software faults is that the user may not be aware of a problem, but in fact some processing may be taking place incorrectly, or in an extreme case information may even be getting lost, without one's knowledge. This is one reason why parallel running is a good idea with new software, as many faults might otherwise be undetected.

The better software suppliers keep users informed by means of a newsletter or similar system so that one is aware when new releases of the software are issued to correct faults; the church can then request an upgrade. This means that if one user has reported a fault, and it has been corrected, all other users will be informed. An important responsibility of the computer co-ordinator is to check such announcements and order new releases. It is very unwise to continue using software that is known to contain bugs.

If there is an optional support scheme for the software, a church needs to be very confident before opting out of the arrangement. Using unsupported software could lead to all kinds of difficulties if a problem is encountered, whether due to a software fault or the user. With software that could have legal implications – such as deeds of covenant or anything that includes statutory reporting – ongoing support is essential.

When software upgrades are offered, the church needs to distinguish between new versions and new releases although different suppliers use the terms in different ways.

In most cases a *new version* offers additional features that make the package easier to use, more flexible, or able to carry out additional functions. Such upgrades are chargeable, and the church must decide whether or not the additional features would be worthwhile. (Unless the software is rarely used, such upgrades are nearly always beneficial: the extra features are often based on requests from existing users; indeed if the church spots an obvious 'gap' in the facilities of a package it is often worth making suggestions for improvement.) In some cases, the supplier may cease to support the old version after a while, so it may be essential to upgrade to the new version at some point, in order for support to be continued.

By contrast, a *new release* (in the terminology of most suppliers) is simply a correction of one or more faults: no additional functions are provided. There is usually no charge for this, or at most a small administrative charge (unless the user is outside any initial guarantee period and has opted out of ongoing support).

There is also an in-between category of upgrade which is a minor change to meet some external requirement. For example, a payroll or deeds of covenant package has to produce information to meet Inland Revenue rules, and if these rules change, the software has to be amended. With payroll packages there are some changes almost every year. There will usually be some charge for this, depending on the complexity of the extra work for the software house.

User groups

A few widely used software packages have user groups which hold meetings from time to time. In such cases it is well worth sparing the time and travel to get involved. The person to attend should be the computer co-ordinator or the senior user of the application concerned. User groups can be a very effective forum of liaison with the supplier in pressing for upgrades and new features, and a great deal is learned through meeting with other more experienced users of the package (although such meetings, unless explicitly billed as training days, can be daunting for very new users). If there seems to be no user group for an important package you are using, you might consider starting one! The supplier can sometimes be persuaded to forward details to other users.

There are also more general user groups for those using computers in specific fields. For church users the main group is the Church Computer Users Group (CCUG), which offers a useful forum and an interesting newsletter discussing all kinds of developments in church computing.

System running costs

In order to ensure the long term dependability of the system, some kind of budget for computer running costs must be available: the size of this will depend very much on the type of maintenance required. It is very much better if the computer co-ordinator can be given authority to spend money from this budget as and when required, rather than having to get individual approval every time a new box of paper is to be ordered.

Items for inclusion in this budget would be:

- hardware maintenance and minor hardware accessories (dust covers etc)

- software support and cost of minor upgrades

- supplies (diskettes, paper, printer ribbons, etc)

- membership of any relevant user groups

- any anticipated ongoing costs for training or travelling.

Points for discussion

1. Why do you think so many users overlook maintenance and backup issues until too late?

2. In a church where several people use the computer, who should be responsible for taking backups? Should each user take backups or should the co-ordinator always take responsibility?

3. *Do not worry about tomorrow* (Matt 6.34).
   The wise ones took containers of oil along with their lamps (Matt 25.4).
   What insight do you feel these passages offer to any consideration of possible problems with computer systems?

9
People and computers in the church ⎯⎯⎯⎯⎯⎯⎯⎯⎯⎯

At first sight, many of the preceding chapters may appear to have been discussing computers and computer technology. But our thesis is that church computing is fundamentally an issue to do with *people*, and the hardware and software are only a means to that end.

Essentially the argument is twofold:

- if a computer system is to be of real service in the church then a high priority must be placed on choosing the right software and hardware which will make that possible

- if the people in the church are to benefit from the use of a church computer system, then issues to do with people must be considered paramount.

This chapter looks at some of the factors which underpin a good relationship between people and computers in the church. Unless that relationship can operate effectively, a computer is unlikely to bring much benefit to the church, and may even cause more harm than good.

Human-computer interaction

It is now widely recognised that computer systems will rarely work unless there is a good interface between the computer and the humans who use it. A computer hobbyist may be prepared to select equipment on technical criteria alone, but for a serious system to be used in a church – or any other organisation – human factors must be regarded as very important.

Human-computer interaction (or HCI) is now a major research area and much has been discovered in the last few years about how to make systems more human oriented, as opposed to machine oriented.

Categories of users

The term *user* has been used in several senses in this book, and it is now important to clarify this. The church as a whole is a user of the computer system; in particular when one uses the term 'data user' in relation to data protection, one is referring to all those who constitute the local church.

Every member or contact of the church is also a user in an indirect way; if such a person receives a newsletter, for example, where the computer has assisted in the production or distribution, then indirectly he or she has been involved in the use of the system. Similarly members may supply information about themselves to be entered on the system, and are involved as users in that sense. Users of this kind are involved in receiving or supplying information.

The church council, minister, and lay leaders may be more closely identified as users. The information they receive from the computer, in the form of printouts or reports may be vital to their decisions or actions. The results of their decisions may be fed back into the system when new ventures are started or when financial decisions are implemented. When subsequent computer results are presented, these users will see the effect of prior decisions. This sort of information system, where the computer and users are involved in a feedback type of exercise can make a major difference to an organisation's strategy. Within the church, the interface between the computer and these key users is thus very important.

The other category of users are those who actually operate the computer, being directly responsible for keying in information, checking details on the screen, and producing printed lists. The way in which operators are able to work with the equipment and the software will greatly affect the efficiency of their work and the extent to which they are able to offer a service to the rest of the church.

The user interface

The human-computer interface is thus a consideration at several levels.

For users who operate the system, important questions include the environment and furniture, the quality and reliability of the hardware, and, in particular the *user-friendliness* of the software. Almost all software nowadays claims to be user-friendly, but this cannot be measured in isolation; it all depends what sort of users are being considered and what they are wanting to do. Software for use in the church should make it easy to enter and amend information, easy to produce the outputs required, and easy to set up and learn, whilst being flexible enough to meet the needs that the church will have. Quality of documentation is very important (and this applies not so much to the quality of print as to the quality and clarity of explanation, the provisions of indexes, diagrams, tutorial and reference sections, and so on). A user who does not really understand the software will be nervous and cautious about making use of the system, and is much more likely to make serious errors.

For the next level of users, those who must take action on the basis of computer produced information (even if that action is only to make some visits), the *presentation* of information is often the most important HCI issue. Some software packages work admirably for recording information on file, but the presentation of their printed listings makes them almost impossible to use. For users directly affected by the computer but who do not actually operate it, their main communication with the system will be in the printed listings they receive: membership lists, financial reports, and so on. (For financial and statistical reports it can sometimes be worth using additional software to allow graphical presentation of information.) If the church wishes to ensure an effective interface between the computer and users in this category, the way that the software produces printed information is a major consideration. (If asking for a software demonstration, one should always insist on seeing the listings the software produces.) Similarly, if such users will generate information to be fed back in to the software, it must be possible for them to specify this clearly and simply to the actual operators.

The third category of users, the ordinary church members, will also be concerned about the presentation and *availability* of information. It is at this level that it is easy to slip up, giving a system which is loved by those with power in the church, and hated by those outside. The computer must never be used as an excuse; if one ever has to say: "I'm sorry I can't tell you; it's on the computer," in response to a question which could formerly be answered immediately, one is failing in the use of the computer as a tool for communication. Church officers need frequent printed listings if they are likely to be asked questions that need instant answers. Quite small details will determine whether or not church members value the information communicated from the computer: adhesive labels, covenant forms, letters, or statements of giving, can make quite a difference to the perception of the computer as something which treats people as humans and not as machines. These factors too are very much determined by the software.

Choice of operators

Although all users will have some effect on the use of the system, a great deal depends on those who will actually operate it. The human-computer relationship, like all relationships, is a two way process: good, user-friendly hardware and software is a big help, but one also needs a computer-friendly human!

For a person to work well with a computer does not in any sense require a detailed understanding of computers or a strong technological orientation, any more than most car users have a detailed understanding of vehicle engineering. But just as driving a car is something that comes more easily to some than to others, so too the use of a computer is influenced by the personality and attitude of the operator (whether minister, secretary, treasurer, or whatever).

It does help if people can have a vague picture in their mind of what the software is doing in accepting information from the keyboard, storing it on disk, and generating outputs. Some people get very confused between the church information being processed, and the software that is causing that processing to take place, and users do need to get concepts such as this clear in their minds. Similarly, an appreciation of the difference between the hardware, the operating system, and the application software, should be included as part of any training.

There is no doubt that a few individuals have a certain 'techno-fear' about any kind of machinery, and these people will take a lot longer than others to become happy with use of a computer. Older people, too, will generally take longer to get to grips with a computer, particularly if they have not even used a typewriter, just as all skills take longer to acquire when one is older. It is usually asking too much for a retired person to reach the understanding needed to be computer co-ordinator, but older people may in time acquire the skills to use one specific application effectively.

Experience with a typewriter is quite useful, not so much in terms of keyboard speed (although this can be helpful) but because typing requires one to think about characters, page sizes, line spacing, and so on – concepts which are relevant in many computer applications. Also, the sort of person who naturally thinks in terms of organised lists and procedures will adapt to the use of a computer much more quickly than someone who prefers an informal approach to everything.

The selection of those people who will actually operate the system must thus be made with care in appreciating the skills different individuals can offer. Their actual work for the church (whether paid or voluntary) might change quite radically, and support at the human level is very important, even if it is just having someone they can turn to who is concerned to see the system used well, to whom they can address complaints when difficulties arise.

Very often, churches ask the impossible by expecting people to get to grips with using a computer at the same time as carrying out all their existing responsibilities. If the church wishes to see the computer used well, it must find ways of freeing people to learn to use the system properly, and must manage to respond when users experience problems or difficulties.

Operators and others

If the relationship between the computer and the operator is important, so too is the relationship between the operator and other users of the information held on the computer.

A negative attitude on the part of those who operate the computer towards others in the church is almost certain to prevent the effective use of a system within church life as a whole. This is one reason why this book has argued strongly for a *church* computer system, or if that is impossible, at least a minister's computer system, rather than *ad hoc* use of a computer owned by a member.

Those who have direct access to the computer have a certain power, and they must be trusted in every way. All information generated by the system is dependent on inputs by the operator. Information will only be accurate and up to date if the operators are committed to keeping it that way.

The computer co-ordinator and other users who operate the machine must be willing to offer a *service* to the church: a service of storing and processing information to the best of their ability, in response to church requirements. An exclusive attitude ("this is *my* computer and what happens is totally up to me") offers little scope for the computer system to support improved communication!

Others must likewise respect the task of the operators, and not expect the impossible. Requests for large listings must be made with several hours (or preferably several days) notice. Amendments and additions to information on file should be communicated to the operator in writing: one cannot tell someone a new telephone number at a meeting and expect the operator to remember and enter it correctly on the computer the next day. (Though some computer co-ordinators or church administrators, recognising the problem, go everywhere with a notepad!)

Practicalities of information management

Whether or not the computer system succeeds as a tool for more effective management of information depends heavily on two practical issues:

- whether the system is sufficiently reliable for people to be able to depend on it as a central source of information

- whether people are sufficiently happy about the issues surrounding personal information on computer that they are prepared to allow the system to be used properly.

Many churches never get beyond the computer as a minor administrative tool because people are unwilling to let themselves depend on it, or they are unwilling to keep sufficient information on computer for any really useful results.

It would, of course, be wrong to place much dependence on the computer until the church is confident that the maintenance, support, and backup issues have been properly addressed, and that problems with the system are unlikely to lead to loss or inaccessibility of information. Normally the computer will be used to produce frequent printouts that can be referred to in the event of problems with the equipment. Computerisation does not mean abandoning the use of paper (frequently more paper is produced than before) but it does mean accepting that the computer held information is the main record from which all else derives.

Likewise, it would be wrong (and usually illegal) to keep files of personal information on computer until people are assured that appropriate data protection arrangements have been made. But once such assurances are available it is only right that the system is put to full use, otherwise the church will see little benefit from its investment.

Commitment to the system

A computer system will never be successful – in a church or anywhere else – without commitment. This commitment is needed at various levels.

Those who are to operate the machine must be committed to acquiring the skills to use it well, and then to providing a good service to the church as a whole.

The church council must be committed to making finance available for software and hardware that will meet the church's needs, and for adequate ongoing support. (In a church with uncertain or complex requirements, this may imply a willingness to engage professional assistance.) The council must also be willing to free people for the time necessary to get acquainted with the system, and must be prepared to act sufficiently quickly (using delegated decisions if appropriate) so that developments are not held up.

The church officers must be committed to seeing the system used at the centre of church information management. This may mean giving up personally created systems of record keeping (and receiving listings instead) so that the computer can be used as the central record. There is very little to be gained from using the computer as a backup to someone's manual information which is regarded as the 'official' source.

The church members, though they may not be consulted individually, must trust the church leaders sufficiently to back the decision to use a computer. Their commitment is needed both in providing any additional finance required to buy the system, and in supplying information that may be requested from them in order that central records can be kept. They may also need to accept that certain information, such as newsletters, church accounts, or membership directories, may be presented in a slightly different form from what they had been used to, and it may need some tolerance to see that minor changes of this kind enable the computer to serve as a better tool for the whole local church.

It is not necessary to get every individual in the church to agree before ordering a computer system; indeed many people may be unconvinced until they see the system in use, or may remain indefinitely sceptical. Similarly it will not usually be possible to get all the church council wildly enthusiastic about the idea. But if strong objections remain from key people who would be involved in supplying or using computer-based information, problems are almost certain. Likewise, it is impossible to proceed without reasonable support from those who will be the operators.

Lack of commitment has killed the potential of systems in many organisations, and has led to numerous computers which sit unused in a corner, gathering dust. Without a reasonable degree of commitment, the church is unlikely to see any benefits from its system.

Criteria to proceed

From the analysis above and from points made elsewhere, it is possible to identify some ten criteria which must be satisfied before a church should proceed with a computer as part of its strategy.

Of course this requires education and discussion – those who know little about computers are unlikely to be immediate enthusiasts. It also requires prayer and reflection about the role that a computer system would have within the church.

If some of these criteria cannot be satisfied, it may still be possible to implement a system as a minor administrative tool for use in certain restricted applications, but such a system is very unlikely to have the broader impact on church life for which this book has argued.

1. There must be at least one definite task where the computer would give real benefit by saving time or enhancing ministry. There is no point in having a computer just because it seems like a nice idea.

2. There will usually need to be at least one or two other application areas where a system would offer some benefits; it is rarely possible to justify a church computer system on one application alone.

3. The church must be willing to find the money for a suitable system that will really do the job, with software and then hardware chosen accordingly. An inadequate system chosen to meet an unrealistically low budget will offer little benefit, and may bring quite serious problems if it is too difficult to use or cannot handle the information required.

4. It must be possible to identify suitable persons who would operate the computer on a day to day basis, including one who could take on responsibility as computer co-ordinator.

5. A reasonable number of leading figures in the church must support the proposal and be prepared to use the computer as a basis for managing information and assisting communication. This does not mean they will have to operate it personally, but they cannot ignore it, and they must recognise its importance as a tool.

6. A suitable location must be found, convenient for those who will operate the system.

7. Some sort of implementation plan is required, acceptable to the

church, which makes adequate arrangements for training and entry of data.

8. The church must accept the principle of holding personal data on computer, and a registration under the Data Protection Act must be submitted as soon as real names are to be entered on the system.

9. Clear plans must be formulated to ensure that problems with hardware or software can be overcome, including appropriate provision for running costs. (Such plans may not necessarily be formulated in detail before the system is ordered, but they must be established before the church becomes seriously dependent on the computer.)

10. There must be at least one person who has a genuine grasp of the possibilities, and a reasonably long term commitment to the church concerned, who is willing to steer the process, respond to any difficulties experienced, and get the church to the point where the computer really is bringing benefit. (It is hoped that this book may enable you, the reader, to be that person.)

The computer as a strategic tool

In order to decide whether a computer can be a strategic tool in a church, one has to ask what is the strategy of that church – what are its objects and where is it going – in order to decide whether the computer has a place in that.

Every church would give a slightly different answer, and it is thus impossible to generalise about exactly *how* churches should use computers: the choice of applications, the people to be involved, the siting of the system, and the practical arrangements made will differ quite widely from one church to another.

The task of this book is not to offer general solutions, but to establish criteria for choosing a system and assessing whether it could be used effectively. Such criteria can then be evaluated by churches large and small in many different pastoral situations. No one would suggest that a computer is right for every church. But where it is right, the scope for better communication and improved information management offers possibilities in mission and ministry that few can currently imagine.

Points for discussion

1. What would be the main differences between a computer system acting as a minor administrative aid and a system which served as a tool for church strategy?

2. Who would be the different types of users of a system in your church (i.e. operators, leaders acting on computer information, and members affected indirectly)? How would each group be affected by introducing a computer?

3. Why do so many computer systems fail becuse of lack of commitment? How is it that an organisation can decide to spend a substantial sum of money on a computer but never make the effort to use it effectively?

4. Which of the ten criteria to proceed would still need to be resolved before a computer could be used as a strategic tool in your church? If you already have a computer, can you identify any of these criteria which were not satisfied and which may have caused difficulties?

5. How do you believe computers will affect Christianity in this country over the next 20 years?

Glossary ————————————————

The following explanations of computer terminology may be of assistance to readers unfamiliar with the field. In many cases the terms are discussed further within the text of the book – refer to the index for details.

Backup   The process of taking an extra copy of some information, to guard against the risk of loss of the first copy (used as a noun, verb, and adjective).

Byte   The unit for measuring amounts of information to be stored or processed. A byte is the amount of information required to hold one character. (On all current machines a byte consists of eight binary digits, i.e. eight bits.)

Data   A general term to cover any computer held information, without implying any particular structure or content.

Disk   A magnetic device for long term storage of information in a form easily accessible to the computer. The term includes both hard and floppy disks.

Disk drive   A peripheral device which can record information on a disk and read it back into the computer, as instructed by the software.

Diskette   A low cost disk that can be removed from a disk drive and stored away. Also known as a *floppy disk*.

Floppy disk   See *diskette*.

Hard disk   A fully enclosed disk and disk drive which can be used to store large amounts of information, also known as a *Winchester*. A hard disk cannot normally be removed from the computer.

Hardware   Physical parts of a computer system: processor, screen, printer etc – all the electronic and mechanical items.

HCI   Human-computer interaction.

I/O   Abbreviation of *input and/or output*.

Input   Transfer of information into the computer (used as a verb and noun).

Kilobyte   Abbreviation: kb or K. A thousand bytes (or 1024 bytes to be precise).

Mainframe computer   A large computer requiring its own machine room with air conditioning and specialised operators. Mainframes are used by large organisations and often support hundreds of terminals.

Megabyte   Abbreviation: Mb. A million bytes (or 1 048 576 bytes to be precise).

Microcomputer   A computer in which the processor is contained on a single electronic chip.

Monitor   The display screen which forms a part of any personal computer.

Operating system   Software which controls the whole computer. The OS must be present before any application program can run. MSDOS is a common example (trademark of Microsoft Corp).

Output   Transfer of information out of the computer (used as a verb and noun).

Parallel running   Operation of old and new systems at the same time in order to compare results.

Peripheral   Peripheral devices are items of hardware which function under the control of the processor to transfer information to or from the latter. There are three categories:
- *input peripherals* take information from a human user into the processor, e.g. a keyboard
- *output peripherals* take information from the processor and convert to a human form, e.g. a printer
- *storage peripherals* provide long term storage of information, e.g. a disk drive.

Personal computer   A common type of microcomputer which includes a screen, keyboard and disk drive(s), which sits on a table and can be used by one person at any time.

Processor   The heart of the computer – also known as the *central processing unit* (CPU). The processor is the part that has the ability to carry out the instructions contained in programs.

Software Programs used to instruct a computer system to carry out specific tasks.

Software package A program or collection of programs sold to many different users.

Spreadsheet A particular kind of software which can be used for planning and calculation of numerical information in rows and columns.

System This is a very general word used in many senses. The main uses in this book are:

- *a computer system* – the complete collection of hardware and software used by a particular organisation
- *an application system* – the software for a particular application
- *an information system* – the overall process by which a given organisation handles information, by human and computer.

Terminal A peripheral device which enables a user to communicate with a computer that is some distance away. The most common type of terminal is a *visual display unit* (VDU) which comprises a screen and keyboard.

Word processing The use of a computer or similar equipment to prepare, edit, revise, store, and print out written documents. The term also describes software packages for this purpose.

Appendix: Bibliography and useful addresses _____

For further reading

Books

Users Experiences of Church Computer Systems John Bronnert, Michael Jones, Christopher Whelan (Kubernesis Booklets No 3, 1986).
Personal Computer: A New Tool for Ministers Russell H. Dilday Jr (Broadman Press, USA, 1985). Available in Britain from Jay books.
A Computer for Your Church Malcolm Dunlop (SPCK, 1986).
Voluntary Organisations and New Technology Ian Irving (NCVO, 1986).
Fifty Ideas to Finance a Church Computer Sharon and Gareth Morgan (Kubernesis Booklets No 2, 1986).

Periodicals

Church Computer is the newsletter of the Church Computer Users Group. Editor: 22 Woodlands Palmway, Timperley, Cheshire WA15 7QV.
MicroDecision and *Which Computer?* are business microcomputing magazines (available in newsagents) which contain frequent up to date articles for those who wish to learn more about hardware and software.

Useful addresses

Church software suppliers

At the time of writing, the main UK firms offering professionally developed church specific software packages are as follows:

Kubernesis Computing for Churches, 56 Devon Road, Bristol, BS5 9AY.
RGS Consultants, Park Terrace, Kingsland, Leominster, HR6 9SQ.
Root SoftCare Ltd, Mobbs Miller House, Christchurch Road, Northampton, NN1 5LL.

Other contacts

Church Computer Users Group, Membership Secretary: 30 The Crescent, Solihull, West Midlands, B91 1JR.
British Council of Churches, Church Computer Project, 2 Eaton Gate, London, SW1W 9BL.
Office of the Data Protection Registrar, Springfield House, Water Lane, Wilmslow, Cheshire, SK9 5AX.

Index

R185 forms, 34
RAM, 51
Registration under Data Protection
    Act, 115–118
Releases of software, 131
Restoring from backup, 125
Running costs, 132

Sexual information, 111
Sheet feeder, 58
Software, 16, 38
    church-specific, 44–46
    copyright, 48–49
    developers, 43, 63
    evaluation, 46–47
    general purpose, 44–46
    licences, 47–49, 91
    maintenance, 130–132
    packages, 40–42
    selection, 40–49, 120
    suppliers, 59
Spelling checker, 26
Spreadsheet, 33, 44
Standard letters, 28–29
Static electricity, 97
Stewardship of information, 112
Stewardship schemes, 31
Stock control systems, 35

Strategic use of computer, 9, 142
Study, minister's, 89
Subject access, 119–120
Support of software, 130–131

Tape streamer, 126
Tax relief, 84
Techno-fear, 76, 77, 110, 137
Telecommunications, 12
Terminals, 12, 90
Tractor feed, 58
Training, 101–104, 138
Type styles, 25, 58–59

User errors, 123, 124
User friendly software, 136
User groups, 132
Users, 74, 88, 107, 135

Vapourware, 40
Versions of software, 131

Welsh, 27
Wide area network, 92
Word processing, 23–30, 44
Wraparound, 23
WYSIWYG, 25